Kwame Nkrumah
and the Dream of African Unity

Lansiné Kaba

DIASPORIC AFRICA PRESS
NEW YORK

LONDON BOROUGH OF WANDSWORTH	
9030 00006 8167 6	
Askews & Holts	20-Jun-2019
320.54096	£16.00
	WW19005220

This book is a publication of
Diasporic Africa Press
New York | www.dafricapress.com

Copyright @ Diasporic Africa Press 2017

Library of Congress Control Number: 2016963543
ISBN-13 978-1-937-30658-8 (pbk.: alk paper)

KWAME NKRUMAH AND THE DREAM OF AFRICAN UNITY

DEDICATION

To all those who struggled for the unity of Africa and her independence, including Chief Albert Luthuli, Nelson Mandela, Amilcar Cabral, King Muhammad V, Patrice Lumumba, and others.

Lansiné Kaba, Ph.D., is Thomas Kerr Distinguished Career Professor at Carnegie Mellon University in Qatar and former President of the African Studies Association (U.S.A.). He was recipient of the Distinguished Teacher award at the University of Minnesota in Minneapolis, Head of the Department and then Dean of the Honors College at the University of Illinois at Chicago. Dr. Kaba has authored numerous works in English and French, including the *Wahhabiyya , Islamic Reform and Politic in French West Africa, 1945-1960*—this book received the Melville Herskovits Prize for the year's best book in English on Africa; *La Guinée dit "non" au général de Gaulle*; and *Cheikh Mouhammad Chérif et son temps ou islam et société à Kankan, Guinée, 1875-1955*.

CONTENTS

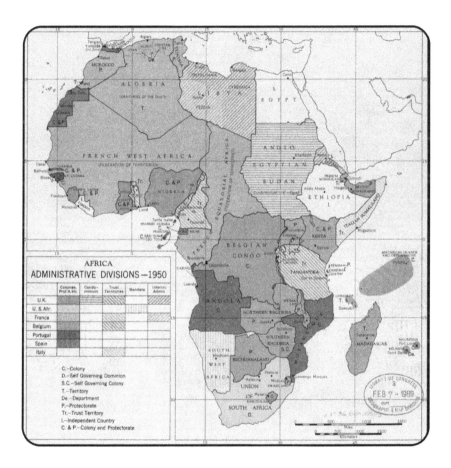

Map of Africa, ca. 1950.

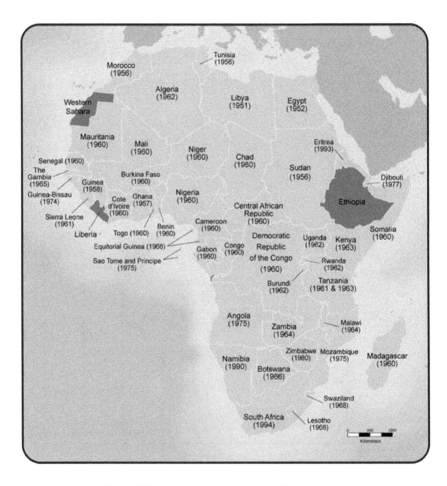

Map of African nations showing date of independence.

PREFACE

Writing about Kwame Nkrumah and the dream of African unity is an exulting task, but also difficult. In effect, the man is complex and the dream is no less so. As he himself confirmed to his personal secretary Erica Powell, "I have no friends, no one really knows me." Like a sphinx, Nkrumah is enigmatic yet captivating, with his thoughts and actions oriented toward African unity.

As a spider is attached to his thread, Nkrumah and his dream of African unity are intimately linked; you cannot separate one from the other. He personifies the quest for unity in the early age of African independence. Today, more than ever, despite narrow nationalism, ethnocentrism, and other obstacles, the wind of change and unity blows across the continent, growing stronger every day, sparing neither region nor country. Now much more than in 1965 when the Organization of Africa Unity (OAU) was created, consciousness of unity entirely encompasses black Africa, even if there are different views about how the framework for coming together should be implemented. As a result, the thoughts of Kwame Nkrumah remain relevant today.

The question remains whether development and unity can be created for the entire continent. And would not such a project be considered utopian? Can Africans realize what the inhabitants of no other continent have ever accomplished? To be realistic, can one conceive of unity between North Africa, which is more or less Arab, and black Africa, south of the Sahara? In any case, the complexity and seriousness of the problem did not seem to discourage the effort towards unity in that period of change.

i

Regional grouping is possible however. In accordance with the resolutions of the first conference of the African people, held in Accra under the aegis of Nkrumah in December of 1958, one could conceive of a certain number of federations covering the greater part of the continent. For example, the Economic Community of West African States (ECOWAS/CEDEAO) was already moving in the direction of true unity by establishing functional supra-national political institutions.

These political events invited Africans to analyze the role of Nkrumah in the quest for African unity. In this domain, the Ghanaian leader remains without compare. Incontestably, he put his energy, his knowledge, and the resources of his country in the service of the fight for independence and unity.

The goal of this work is to study the different stages of the deeds and experiences of Nkrumah in the pursuit of African unity. It is a protracted and exciting work. For embodied in Nkrumah, the dream of unity takes on gigantic proportions. Its journey goes beyond West Africa to encompass the new world, the Congolese forests, the deserts of the Sahara and the great lakes of Central Africa. The dream is understood to be a political, cultural, and historical process.

Far from being a hagiography or a biography, or an essay on the ideology and foreign politics of Nkrumah, this work follows the adventures of the dream, from the years studying across the Atlantic to the Accra Summit in 1965 and the *coup d'état* in 1966. Throughout, the analysis tries to understand the genesis of the dream and the effort required for its realization. These discussions deal with the difficulties of implementing a policy of regrouping at the level of independent states. Thus, we dedicate our study to a specific theme, limited and precise, namely, the saga of unity embodied by Kwame Nkrumah.

Nkrumah's merit lies in his ability to dream the impossible. This is the source of his fame which only increased despite the errors and contradictions of his government. Like a demiurge, Nkrumah and his dream were reborn out of the events that had turned Africa upside down. For the historian, the man represents a paradox. His case demonstrates that in certain situations the result is less important than the idea that aims to create something grand and sublime, which puts humans running towards a better tomorrow. In that regard, it can never be overemphasized the significance of African Unity, to which his name will forever be associated.

To write this work, I did not consult the archives of the countries towards which the African politics of Nkrumah were directed. In Ghana itself, the destruction by soldiers of Nkrumah's library and many historical documents of his regime is an immediate limitation. However, I did use the writings of Nkrumah himself, the commentaries of his adversaries, and the analysis of experts who have examined his policies. In that regard the work of W. Scot Thompson on the foreign politics of Nkrumah, which was based on the documents of the first hours made available to the author immediately after the *coup d'état* in 1966, has proved to be, along with other works, an invaluable source. Clearly, we assume the responsibility for the translation of texts in French.

Every work is the fruit of cooperation. Allie B. S. Kabba procured several Ghanaian journal copies for me as well as many other documents from the archives of Ghana. Basil Davidson offered me a copy of his book on Nkrumah, with pertinent suggestions. Kodjo Yeboah-Sampong proved himself to be an exceptionally versatile assistant: he diligently collected the available texts from the Chicago Area libraries, and enriched our studies with his understanding of Ghana. Without his contribution, this book would never have become exposed so early. Valerie Vines equally put her computer expertise in service of this work.

As usual, the great witness and indisputable aid in the development of this work remains my wife, Fanta, who for weeks sacrificed her sleep to listen, critique and improve my thoughts and my language. To her, and to all my wonderful colleagues, I remain grateful.

The translation of this work into English was made possible by the request of Diasporic Africa Press and the hard work of the translator, Dr. Jeremy Thompson. The final version was the result of Ruqiyyah Nu'Man's excellent editing and translation skills, which, coupled with mine own suggestions and corrections, helped polish the work and prepare it for a new audience.

I

NKRUMAH, THE IDEA OF UNITY AND THE AFRICA OF TODAY

A man, a dream, a destiny that aims to be in the service of Africa and the black world, but is also a tragedy and a source of inspiration. In a phrase, this is the life of Kwame Nkrumah, educator, nationalist and head of state of exceptional importance. As Basil Davidson depicts him, Nkrumah appears like a prophet, who leaves a lasting imprint on his times.[1] He is a paradox. Despite the failure of his policies both within Ghana and globally, he remains popular and captivating.

Although each country has its pantheon of distinguished men and women, for many Africans none of these figures, apart from Nelson Mandela in recent times perhaps, can compare with Nkrumah in the matter of the saga of African unity. Whatever judgment one makes about his regime (for instance, of its fiscal management or of its one-party system), his name symbolizes a dream of promethean scope: the quest for African unity and respect for Africa on the international stage. In many respects, his political activity can be summed up as a continuous struggle to achieve the dream of unity. The open-mindedness, generosity and perseverance that characterized this movement have not ceased to make an impression.

Like the names Patrice Lumumba and Nelson Mandela, Nkrumah captivates the peoples of Africa and the progressives of the world. He counts among the great leaders of the twentieth century, who are often oblivious of the present while concerning themselves with the future. Nkrumah personifies that great movement of liberation and unity without which Africa risks remaining on the margin of modern history. His name is synonymous with independence within unity. How did a child from the small village of Nkroful in the far southwest of Ghana become the symbol of this crusade?

From his years of study in the United States of America to the glorious years of Ghana's independence and to the bitterness of exile at Conakry, Guinea, the question of independence and of African unity haunted Kwame Nkrumah. A veritable obsession, the vision remained of a united Africa, independent, great, and powerful, without borders and without the other barriers inherited from colonialism. Such was the dream. But was it an illusion? A chimera? A fantasy? Was this dream not the fruit of a fertile imagination and far ahead of its time? Could this dream be achieved? Whatever the answer, Nkrumah consecrated his entire life to it.

Formal education and the "school of life" helped the young Kwame to develop himself. To some degree, he followed the example of his older contemporary, Dr. Nnamdi Azikiwe, champion of unitary nationalism in Nigeria, who, moreover, encouraged him to pursue his studies in the United States.[2] Nkrumah became aware of the dream of unity on the benches of universities, in the cafés and churches of black ghettos in Philadelphia and New York, far from the Akan lands of the Gold Coast where he was born one Saturday, and far too from the European metropolises which apportioned Africa for themselves after the Berlin Conference in 1885.

Nkrumah advocated the idea of unity in London, where he led the life of a Pan-African activist. Experience abroad strengthened his idealistic and romantic tendency. He adopted unity as the doctrine of his party, the Convention People's Party (CPP), which led the struggle for independence in the Gold Coast, his country, to which he gave the name of the ancient empire of Ghana. He generously placed the resources of Ghanaian independence in the service of African liberation.

After Guinea's vote in the referendum held by General De Gaulle in France and her colonies in 1958, Nkrumah came to the aid of Guinea's young government and formed the Ghana-Guinea Union.

When the Federation of Mali was broken up between Senegal and the Sudanese Republic due to French manipulation, he jumped to the aid of the new republic of Mali. Along with the presidents Sékou Touré and Modibo Keïta, he created the Ghana-Guinea-Mali Union, which he conceived as the precursor to a Union of the African States. He energetically supported Patrice Lumumba and the legal government of the Congo (Zaire). Like a pilgrim, he traveled from capital to capital to convince his peers of the necessity of a continental government.

Just after Ghana's independence, Nkrumah organized the first Conference of Independent African States, as well as the first All-African Peoples' Conference to establish the idea of unity. Without reserve he encouraged student organizations and gave aid to liberation movements to hasten the process of independence. Several years later, despite vast differences with his peers, he accepted the creation of the Organization of African Unity (OAU) at Addis Ababa. The OAU seemed to him to be a step in achieving his grand dream.

Nkrumah's African policy aimed to promote independence and to assure the unity of African states by means of a continental government. In the face of the rising interference of foreign powers in African affairs, he aimed to resolve African problems, such as Congo's crisis, within an African context and through Africans themselves, with the assistance of the United Nations. Based on a principle of neutrality, his foreign policy was anti-colonialist and anti-racist. Nkrumah wanted to forge a consensus between the independent states about the critical issues of the times and thus prepare the conditions for unity.

In the eyes of the Ghanaian leader, unity was necessary for Africa to be able to develop and to enjoy its independence in freedom, and the respect of the law. That was his creed. Despite the pitfalls which marked his path, and despite blunders in executing his dream, he did not cease to believe in it: that was his life's goal. Would he succeed? This was the question. Whatever the case, he launched a challenge to his generation, to ours, and to generations to come.

THE NEED FOR UNITY

In the second half of the twentieth century, the search for unity has been a feature of global conscience. Despite Malthusian arguments, a close link seems to exist between development and the size of modern states. Surface area and demography represent a certain advantage for the long-term development of nations. For instance, Brazil, India, China, and other large countries of the so-called Third World have met with undeniable success in their plans for development despite difficulties in their structural order.

It is now a truism to emphasize the role of demographics and space in the economic rise of the United States; western Europe struck out on the path towards unity in 1992, despite the reluctance of the British right wing; and as further confirmation of this observation, the countries of North Africa (the Maghreb) have collaborated increasingly with the aim of presenting a united front against the Europe of 1992. Are not the East Asian countries also trying to unify and work together as a protective measure? But what can one say of black Africa?

Africa faces a lack of unity and democracy. The problem is crucial since unity in a democracy leads to growth and development by encouraging private initiatives. Democracy can also lead to well-informed and efficient participation of the state in economic life. The failure of states and the lack of unity make development uncertain. This weakness and uncertainty are at the source of both the general decline in Africa's global position and the numerous prejudices directed against it.

For example, over the course of the year 1990, black Africa was paraded through the headlines in Parisian media.[3] (Let us call the continent by the name "black Africa," since these reports omitted the Maghreb.) The written press, adopting a common front that is seldom equaled, launched an assault on black Africa, "the world's sick child." And what articles they wrote! The titles are provocative and the content pessimistic, disclosing a certain mentality. One such review showed "The collapse of Africa," another "Afro-pessimism." The well-respected *Le Monde* itself asks, "What to do with black

Africa?" With a mocking tone and poor taste, another such magazine exclaims, "Black kings and bad whites—why Africa is splitting open." *The Express* has dedicated a special issue to "Africa, shipwreck of a continent."

For much of these French polemicists, of whom some have not been so bold as to identify themselves, Africa is a condemned, if not cursed, world. This fatalistic opinion has become a leitmotif in mainstream as well as in educated circles. According to the *Express*, Africa is "worrisome," "requires advice" and is "disturbed." But whom does this worry? What advice is needed? And whom does this disturb? The diagnoses of the wounds of black Africa are legion. It is useful to expose them in order to eradicate the evil. But is this the purpose of these reports?

It is an incontestable fact that the track record of African independence is partly negative. But, to draw it up in catastrophic terms, in a language where polemic is greater than calm reflection, is an obstacle. The condescension of the polemicists and the venom of their attacks, not only against the leaders but also against Africa and Africans, revive an old colonialist if not racist mentality. Indeed, what should one think of an "expert" who has doubts about Africa because of the "lymphatic temperament" of its peoples? This is Albert Mannoni resurrected, together with his notorious psychology of the colonized!

With a nearly inconceivable hostility, another author advises France to carry out its priorities in Europe and Asia and to abandon "the little republics on a medicated drip, without past, without future, corrupt and vagrant." Upon reading these articles, one would gladly exclaim, "Long live Raymond Cartier," and his anti-African doctrine known by the name of "Cartierism," which has made the magazine *Paris-Match* well-known and problematic since the 1950s!

In contrast with these writings, a rigorous analysis can denounce the collapse of regimes without also attacking the identity of its peoples. The lack of objectivity and honesty discredits these articles. Truth in good faith is constructive, while condescension and contempt under the cover of truth disclose bad faith. To criticize African leaders for their incompetence, their corruptness, and their other faults may be legitimate. But to spread contempt for Africans serves to reveal attitudes that are regrettable and dishonorable.

Quite often, many critics of Africa took advantage of their expertise concerning Africa, be it French, international, or African. Some assumed very important functions as advisors to the "black kinglets" or international experts or representatives of important fiscal concerns. They then form part of the problem, and know full well where "the rub is." There is no corruption without corrupters. In general, the foreign expert unfortunately refuses to assume his responsibilities, making dialogue difficult.

Black Africa suffers from evils of all kinds, from dictatorship to malnutrition to AIDS. It is far from both realizing its economic potential and from satisfying its peoples' fundamental needs. Everywhere, almost without exception, civil or military despotism suffocates liberty, flouts justice and thus sows poverty. The ethic of work and of responsibility gives way to incompetence and irresponsibility. Unity is still only a word. For national integration, "ethnocracy" and nepotism may have to be substituted—they are expressions of narrow and regressive regionalism. The lure of easy gain has corrupted the ruling leaders as well as those who are ruled. Everywhere, corruption reigns supreme.

THE CRISIS OF AFRICAN INSTITUTIONS

Though depressing, this negative impression justifies neither fatalism nor pessimism. The problem is political, and therefore can be resolved, as Nkrumah thought. In his dual role as intellectual and political leader, he highlighted the inadequacies and weaknesses of African states. For him, it is not Africa which is condemned, but rather the regimes as they exist now; in other words, as they have been fashioned and directed by the colonial and neo-colonial system.[4] This is the problem, and it bears on the question of democracy and unity.

Objectively, the crisis of Africa is one of institutions and the men in place. For example, on one hand, there are institutions from former days that have become invalid, and on the other hand, there are modern institutions ill adapted to African conditions and that are incapable of generating long-term development. It is difficult for such a contradiction to lead to progress. Thus, for reasons at once inherent to their nature and characteristic of the style of exercising power, African states in their present forms are functioning poorly and to produce mediocre results.

The present situation is the result of the conditions under which countries have attained independence. Though colonization is not responsible for all the present ills affecting Africa, it is certain that the structures inherited from colonialism lack viability. For instance, in 1958 France destroyed the federations of western Africa and French Equatorial Africa to give birth to states without dynamic infrastructures. England rejected the possibility of a democratic union between both the territories of East Africa and the member countries of the Federation of Rhodesia to encourage the formation of a multitude of independent states whose economy is funneled toward South Africa. It must be said that it was a little too late when General De Gaulle himself recognized this fundamental inadequacy (of the independent states) which makes modern Africa the target of conflict and easy prey for seeds that sow weakness and destruction.[5]

Paradoxically, Africa experiences an imbalance between its resources, its social aspirations, and its institutions. For example, although it is a continent where much of the population is rural, it spends a good part of its meager resources on importing rice, flour, and other foodstuffs for feeding itself. How can you expect a state that can barely assure its alimentary needs to develop? African states suffer from the incapacity to develop what already exists. As Basil Davidson emphasizes, one is entitled to wonder if "Africa will be able to survive" in its current form.[6]

Davidson's question suggests that one examine the achievements of independent African states since their independence. For example, in the areas of education, health, and communication, one observes a growth whose rates, though still modest, are higher than that achieved during the colonial period. The mortality rate has decreased a little bit everywhere, and the population is growing, with certain consequences. The growth is still more spectacular in sectors that export agricultural products and ores. This record deserves to be emphasized.

Nevertheless, the problem remains serious. Many countries have faced a severe budget crisis. The structural modifications imposed by donors and multilateral institutions like the World Bank and the International Monetary Fund seem to create more unemployment than well-being. The crisis is exacerbated by the survival of colonial structures and the lack of control on export product prices.

One can say, as Nkrumah did, that development in the present context is nearly impossible. Even worse, the states which are generally small and fragile compete with one another. In addition, their leaders often confuse the public's money for their own. A lack of political morality causes corruption and the illegal accumulation of wealth. These are the scourges that weaken the African system by discouraging both the foreign investor and the local entrepreneur.

And so, black Africa suffers. As the preceding remarks show, the current political and economic domain is condemned to be in crisis. More than every African leader of his age, despite the collapse of his own administration, Kwame Nkrumah reflected on this problem. In his autobiography and in his writings on neo-colonialism, the Congo crisis, and the need for unity, he methodically made a diagnosis about the burning problems with which Africa was confronted. In clear language, he demonstrated how institutional weakness undermines standing regimes. In addition, he analyzed how the inequality between industrialized countries and countries that produce raw materials contributed to stagnation and crisis in Africa.

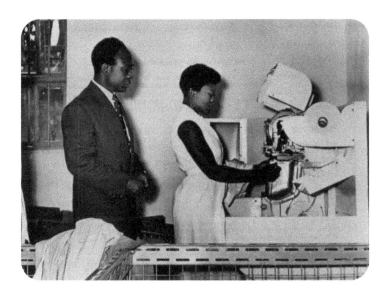

Dr. Kwame Nkrumah, the Prime Minister of the Gold Coast,
watches an operator at work on a machine producing metal labels
in a factory set up under the auspices of the Industrial Develop-
ment Corporation of the Gold Coast.

This is why it is difficult today to envisage development in Africa.
Indeed, unlike the sectoral growth which was mentioned above,
development presumes a continuous self-propelling growth. Such
advance is comprehensive, multifaceted, and long-term and proceeds
with the actualization of liberty. It implies the development of all the
living conditions of the people for themselves in the inescapable and
irreversible trajectory of progress. Development suggests a qualitative
transformation in all areas of life. The absence of this possibility explains the need for African unity.

Hence, we arrive at the significance of Nkrumah's dream. Today,
much more than in the first years of independence, Africans feel
the need to create the real conditions for development. Centered on
Africans, self-sufficient, and long-term, this work implies integration
and freedom, unity, and democracy. To this end, Africans are dealing
with a Promethean struggle that demands discipline and perseverance and that presupposes confidence in their own value. Nkrumah's

actions are intelligible in light of this imperative. For him, the material and cultural well-being of the peoples of Africa demand unity.

CULTURE AND UNITY

All Africans are aware of the lack of unity, but the interests at stake and the men in place slow the process of regroupment. With the *coup d'état* led by Colonel Kotoka and Commander Afrifa who named General Ankrah to power, a coup that most observers attributed to the role of the CIA, Nkrumah's crusade reached its end.[7] The dream, however, did not disappear, nor, moreover, can it disappear.

Today, many events confirm Nkrumah's accuracy of vision. Leaders change, but regimes have fundamentally remained the same. Poverty persists and influence by foreign powers remains dominant. This is why Africans everywhere stand up to their governments; and this is no plot. Obviously, these actions denote no plots against standing regimes, but there is a popular will to make Africa move and "to end the shame and poverty." The leaders must acknowledge that "the present condition cannot continue."

Tyranny and autocracy must disappear and yield to democracy. A one-party system, or the total absence of a party, or the imposition of two official parties can no longer be justified. The meager resources must not be squandered either in armament and secret police or prestige expenses or the maintenance of the presidential court. Honesty and transparency must replace greed. In the face of so serious a crisis, Africa can no longer be silent or accept blind submission.

Thus, the "wind of change" blows with greater and greater velocity and increasingly powerful strength. Rich or poor, literate or illiterate, Africans are refusing "traditional explanations" and are demanding change. They are refusing to be considered infants to be bottle fed. The people of Africa are developed, ready to assume their responsibilities and to take over. The revolt against injustice and arbitrariness has become a powerful expression of modern African culture.

The media itself, despite its submission to the state apparatus, does contribute, paradoxically, to the growing cultural unity across borders. Business men and women cross these borders carrying news and goods, along with their sentiments about the narrowness of the economic conditions, all of these under the severe eye of customs officers. To all appearances, only the civil servants remain fixed, enmeshed in the straitjackets of "national" administrations. Despite many contradictions, the states themselves are waking up from their lethargy, as evidenced by the activity of inter-African institutions like the African Development Bank and the Economic Community of West African States, which, in order to respond to the challenge, must equip themselves with efficient political institutions.

More interesting still is the reawakening of Africa from the "depths of torpor" in which narrow nationalism would have it stagnate. The masses are growing impatient and demanding concrete results. This Africa, which suffers no inferiority complex, is healthy and vigorous, despite its appearance of fatigue. Aware of the limits of the small states as well as of the poor management of its legacy, it aspires to freedom and prosperity in the open and wants to get off the ground safely to build its future in unity. This aspiration belongs to the whole continent.

The march towards union corresponds to one of the characteristics of black Africa's history, as a broad outline of its past affirms. Despite the strength of ethnic sentiment (a universal sentiment insofar as one always belongs to a group or region), the great precolonial states have included different populations and have worked towards creating political structures in a unitary trend. The experience of Africans of the diaspora, let us note, runs similarly and as a result exercises an influence on pan-African sentiment. As Nkrumah observed, the New World is for blacks a land of suffering and hope. This dualism led him to dream, more so than his peers, of unity as a process of salvation to be realized on the basis of culture and politics.

But is unity a myth or a potential reality? To answer this question, it is necessary to consider certain anthropological ideas. Apart from the people of the Maghreb, who are Arab or Berber and generally oriented toward the Middle East, Africans of the tropics are recognized in the first place by their physical traits. However much they are assimilated to foreign cultures, they cannot escape this reality. Their color determines the way they are perceived at first approach and, in certain conditions, even their social position.

Is it necessary to recall that under the colonial regime one obtains everything not based on one's intrinsic merit but of their "race"? Skin color prevails over ethnicity, as the experience of Africans living abroad shows. In Paris, as in Moscow, one is not Wolof, Fula, or Baule: one is simply black and African; in New York, as in Washington or Beijing, one is not even Guinean or Angolan or Tanzanian, one is simply black and African. Subjectively, contact with western culture leaves an imprint on Africans. Africans are identified on the basis of their difference from Europeans and Asians. Color matters.

Concretely, however, the sense of unity rests on tangible features. Despite differences of language, religion and customs, there are cultural elements that unite Africans. The sense of family and of authority, the awareness of the afterlife, rites of passage, agricultural systems, and artistic traditions—these are common features of African societies. In this respect, any study that underlines Africa's diversity instead of its unity or that is unaware of the historical foundations of African nationalism is debatable.[8]

African nationalism is a concept based on history and feeling as well as an idea to be carried forward. It also rests on the community of interest vis-à-vis Europe. In all cases, Africans must "wear their black coat with pride" and build their world. Such is the profound sense of awareness of unity in Nkrumah. For him, unity remains a powerful ideology of liberation and development. Whether he succeeded in realizing his dream, his experience is a source of inspiration for the Africa of today, which searches for self, which suffers, and which aspires to better tomorrows.

2

PAN-AFRICANISM OR THE GENESIS OF THE DREAM

THE VISION ON BOARD THE SHIP

In May 1945, Kwame Nkrumah, a student from the Gold Coast, embarked from New York for Liverpool, England. He was filled with joy and emotion. He was delighted to complete the studies that he had begun ten years earlier in difficult circumstances. What a long journey and what an experience! It was the answer of the prayers of his mother and his elders, a victory of will over adversity, for which he thanked God. He was happy to see so many friends, Americans and Africans, coming out to accompany him to the port. What a difference from when he landed at the same port in 1935, a foreigner alone, his only reference a scrap of paper with the address of an expatriate from Sierra Leone in Harlem, the black neighborhood of New York![9] Since then, his horizon had expanded. He was moved. Slowly, out of joy, he began to cry.

The siren sounded signaling departure. The ship raised the anchor, and slowly made its way out to open sea. The hands rose one last time, and little by little, the quay disappeared. To impress on his mind the last image of the United States, which had so fascinated him, the traveler gazed upon the scene that stretched out beyond the port; watching the vanishing outline of the skyscrapers which had made New York such a spectacular city.

Suddenly, atop an immense concrete boulder, rising from the distance was a great, white lady, dressed in a Grecian peplum, her head crowned with laurels, her raised arm brandishing a torch. The Statue of Liberty! The great lady's gesture was a farewell sign, the young African thought. And so, he answered her in a scarcely audible voice, saying: "Hail to you, Beautiful Lady, who opened my eyes and showed me the profound significance of liberty. Be assured: I shall carry your message to Africa."[10]

The Prime Minister of the Gold Coast, Dr. Kwame Nkrumah, is received by Vice-Admiral Sir Peveril William-Powlett when paying a courtesy visit to HMS Euryalus in the Accra roads.

On the ship that took him to England, Nkrumah could not free himself from that image. She was with him, everywhere, in his cabin, at the restaurant, on the bridge. In this moving world of the boat, without apparent segregation, the image of the Lady with the torch forcefully appeared to him, and merged with two precise visions.

What were the two ideas on which the mind of the solitary traveler focused? The first, without being entirely new, did not lack for power or interest. The expression of a genuine historical awareness, it went back to the last years of independence of African kingdoms at the end of the nineteenth century. It was the image of black resistance against white invaders and conquerors. A genuine Akan, just like the Baule, the Anyi, and the Abron of Côte d'Ivoire (Ivory Coast), he remembered Prempeh I, the Asantehene, king of the great Asante confederation whose capital was Kumase. He had been defeated and exiled by the English in 1896. Nkrumah also recalled the deeds of Samori Toure, great conqueror and resistance-fighter of the Sudanese-Guinean savannahs, who left an impact on the peoples of the Gold Coast.[11] Nkrumah could not forget that Prempeh and Samori had envisioned forming a common front against the European conquerors. He recalled too the action of many other sovereigns whose names stood on the noble pages of African history in the late nineteenth century, which had been so full of historical significance for the black world.

For the solitary traveler, this first vision called more than ever for the liberation of Africa, which was divided and colonized. Unlike the builders of empire and the heroes of the resistance, he thought, his generation had a weapon available to them that was as powerful and dangerous as that of the colonizer. This weapon was modern education, which he had just spent ten years of his life, far from his birthplace, to obtain. Knowledge, he reckoned, is the source of nobility for the individual and for society. The modern school was conceived as the new battlefield where the destiny of Africa and the black world was being played out, and from which Africans must know how to borrow without losing themselves, as he had studied in his sociology and education courses at the University of Pennsylvania. The school represented an effective weapon, and he expressed a wish to one day develop education in the Gold Coast.

Ghana's Prime Minister Kwame Nkrumah, receiving award from
University of Pennsylvania Vice-Provost Roy Nichols, ca. 1958
(University of Pennsylvania Archives, Alumni Records Collection
Box 1931).

Moreover, the traveler Nkrumah considered another advantage available to his generation. After 1885, he recalled, an arrogant and powerful Europe had conquered Africa. But he observed that at present, in 1945, the situation was different. Though victorious over Hitler's Germany, France and England were weakened. In addition, they owed much to the war effort of the African colonies. He felt that a reform of the colonial regime was possible. Moreover, Nkrumah knew better than most of his generation that without the United States' participation, victory over German forces would have been difficult.

Yet, despite its bold capitalism and virulent racism, the United States had an anti-colonial tradition, as emerged from reading the Declaration of Independence, a key document of the American Revolution. In this context, it became apparent why, after President Franklin Roosevelt, President Harry Truman pressured Winston

Churchill to decolonize.[12] Nkrumah concluded that from this point on, it was the responsibility of Africans to organize themselves like the peoples of Asia and the Middle East in order to win their independence and begin the development of their continent. He intended to dedicate himself to this task. It would be his mission.

The second idea that nagged at Kwame on the liner—a still grander one—had to do with Africa's future, and specifically with its future in unity and in dignity. Paradoxically, this idea had American origins. Nkrumah became aware of it at school when he decided to obtain degrees in sociology and economy at Lincoln University, a black institution, and at the well-known University of Pennsylvania, which had been founded by the philosopher and statesman Benjamin Franklin. Marxism helped him to become familiar with the origin of modern colonialism and imperialism. He devoured books on the great historical and sociological questions to satisfy his intellectual curiosity and to appreciate better the causes of the United States's growth. The African student had tried for a long time to explain to himself why a new state like the USA had managed to develop and surpass Europe.

It is a very interesting question. American power, he learned, derived in concrete terms from the abundance of its resources and from its demographic weight. The student noted with pleasure how rich too his birthplace Africa was. Was there not another explanation, perhaps more pertinent? Nkrumah recalled his history lectures.

The remarkable thing about the English colonies of North America in 1776 was the political consensus forged by the rebels despite differences of region, temperament, religion and even ideology. The same rebels would become the founding fathers of the American nation. Indeed, there was clear divergence between the South's rural and slave economy and the North's bourgeois-mercantile economy. And what a difference between the group of Thomas Jefferson, Benjamin Franklin, John Adams, and James Madison—disciples of enlightened philosophers—and the group of George Washington and other plantation lords who were not very concerned with intellectual questions. And yet by surmounting personal pettiness, they managed to get along and to create the first modern republic based on a constitutional document.[13]

What was the lesson for Nkrumah, an African student interested in philosophy and in development? Standing on the ship deck, soothed by the warm air of spring, amid the free and vast horizon, Kwame dreamed of the United States of Africa, a future giant that would restore dignity to blacks. As if to comfort himself, with a smile on his lips, he remembered his debates with Nigerian students and how Lenin's analysis of underdevelopment helped him to get the idea of unity adopted by the Association of African Students in Pennsylvania.[14] He was already sketching out a plan that, he hoped, would bring about unanimity among African leaders when the occasion presented itself.

For the traveler, it was difficult to forget "the other America," that of blacks and of the underprivileged. Poor student that he was, he knew the suffering of the "wretched of the earth"[15] and of the "social rejects" within the United States. He also had had fruitful contacts with different organizations and was given courses on African American history at Lincoln and at Philadelphia. From his discussions with the members of W. E. B. Du Blois's National Association for the Advancement of Colored People (NAACP), the Urban League and Marcus Garvey's Universal Negro Improvement Association (U.N.I.A), he remembered the feelings of admiration and pride that they felt for Africa, the unknown land of their forefathers.

Despite the hostility between Garvey and Du Bois, their doctrines complemented one another. Each in his way left a considerable influence on the young man from the Gold Coast. Faithful to this education, the traveler imagined himself dressed in a beautiful outfit of *kente* cloth, the ceremonial clothing for Akan and Ewe peoples of his region, while welcoming his brothers and sisters of the diaspora to Accra. He entered onto the path of activist pan-Africanism and wanted to make it a doctrine in the search and service of liberation and unity. And so, his thoughts flew away toward the great men whose actions distinguish the history of pan-Africanism.

PAN-AFRICANISM AND THE ORIGIN OF THE DREAM OF UNITY

Nkrumah's dream of unity derived in part from his American experience and contact with activist and radical cells from the black community of Philadelphia and New York. These two experiences, one academic and the other political and human, led him on the path of pan-Africanism and unity of all black people. To understand his context, it is necessary to sketch the pan-African cultural current that shook the black world on both sides of the Atlantic starting from the nineteenth century.

To begin with, we are dealing with a movement of American inspiration, contrary to the opinions of many Francophone writers. For free Blacks of the diaspora were better informed about political and cultural events that vexed Europe in the nineteenth century. From the Rhine in Germany to the Volga in Russia, politicians, writers, and artists have all considered the problems of nationalism and unity. Pan-Germanism, pan-Slavism, Zionism and many others have been new expressions that indicate consciousness of common origin and affective bonds.

Very early, the literate black people of the diaspora took an interest in this debate through their contacts with Central European nationals who immigrated to American cities. Thus, little by little, a rapport developed between currents of thought hailing from Europe and the currents emerging from the conditions in black communities. Confirming this contact, the expression "pan-Negroism" emerged, though it was quickly abandoned for the term "pan-Africanism," which should be noted, is much more appropriate on a cultural level.[16] What are the foundations of this current of thought?

Historians do not agree on the exact date of the genesis of pan-Africanism, but this is not important. What is significant is to discover the historical context that resulted in such awareness. It is necessary then to start not from Africa, the motherland of blacks, nor from the Americas, the lands of their exile, but rather from a small area, which is nevertheless one of great importance. This spot is located between the two banks of the Atlantic, in the middle of the sea, in the inferno of the slave ships.

The ocean crossing, generally known as the "middle passage," is a nightmare that lasted an average of forty to sixty days, a journey without a return and to a destination unknown to the "passengers." Let us imagine the sailing ships, overloaded with its crew, provisions, and the human cargo in the bottom of the haul. Chained two by two at the wrists and ankles, the "passengers" were stretched out naked like a parquet floor, groaning from hunger, cold, pain and homesickness. Men, women, and children, each separated in the hold, were united by their color and their miserable condition. It was an awful spectacle. The living, dead and dying lay in this dark world, polluted by blood, vomit, excrement, vermin, and rats. With good reason the poet Robert Hayden and the novelist Alex Haley have given the crossing the name "voyage through life and death," which disembarks on distant and unknown banks.[17] This traumatizing and inhuman world is the birthplace of the first feeling of unity among the children of Africa, uprooted from their land.

Pan-Africanism is based on a concrete and psychological experience that was lived out. Beginning from this feeling of dreadful pain, the experience has transformed into an active awareness. The slaves did not let themselves be carried across without resistance. Formidable mutinies often brought death to enslavers and slaves. Paradoxically, the fear of the chained slave felt by the crew, which was armed with rifles, made the crossing still more cruel. Africans saw their brothers declared dangerous and then tortured before being thrown alive to the sharks.

Revolts on board the ships, a symbol of courage and heroism, produced the first movement of unity and supplied the source of the first burst of pan-Africanism. There, against the white traders and sailing toward an unknown destiny, blacks of all origins joined hands. Mandinka, Susu and Fula, Wolof and Serer, Akan and Ewe, Yoruba, Igbo, and Hausa, Bakongo and Baluba—all felt a common solidarity and launched an assault on their common enemy.

Belonging to the black race cemented their unity. In other words, for the black leaders of the diaspora, a tragic consciousness of black identity was linked to the experience at sea. Being faithful to the heroic tradition of their chained ancestors, they would try to germinate this awareness into a doctrine of cultural and political regeneration and unity.

Arriving empty-handed on the banks of the New World, the survivors of the crossing retained only a memory of their native land. For them, Africa was henceforth simply an abstraction, a paradise lost, as the poems of Countee Cullen and other writers of the diaspora show.[18] In many respects, existence under the slave regime was a continuation of the brutality of the Atlantic crossing. It was a new life, having no direct contact with African culture, a life uprooted and alienated. But it was also a painful experience of assimilation, adaptation, and synthesis between African and European values on American soil. According to the historian John Blassingame, the African, though being Americanized, ended up Africanizing America.[19]

Because of the importance of race in the New World's culture, the black elite of the diaspora sought to rediscover the essence of its identity. Its members spoke to the motherland that they did not know. They reclaimed their black identity by revalorizing the sullied image of Africa and by dreaming of a dignified future and union with their African brothers. Pan-Africanism carried a profound and powerful emotion, as the sonnet of Claude McKay says:

> For the dim regions whence my fathers came.
> My spirit, bandaged by the body, longs.
> Words felt, but never heard, my lips would frame;
> My soul would sing forgotten jungle songs.
> I would go back to darkness and to peace,
> But the great western world holds me in fee,
> And I may never hope for full release
> While to its alien gods I bend my knee.
> Something in me is lost, forever lost,
> Some vital thing has gone out of my heart,
> And I must walk the way of life a ghost
> Among the sons of earth, a thing apart.
> For I was born, far from my native clime,
> Under the white man's menace, out of time.[20]

For Claude McKay, awareness of Africa required taking a stance against slavery, the slave trade and Europe. That was one of the conditions of liberating black people. In this way, it found a common destiny with Africans. This conviction also emerges prominently in the poetry of Langston Hughes, who lived in Africa:

> We are related—you and I.
> You from the West Indies,
> I from Kentucky.
> We are related—you and I.
> You from Africa,
> I from these States.
> We are brothers—you and I.[21]

Brotherhood implies a feeling of solidarity and pride, and even a challenge, such as the one Hughes launches against those who are ignorant of the value of black pigmentation:

> I am a Negro:
> Black as the night is black
> Black as the depths of my Africa[22]
> In this way, black people entered the path of their liberation.

The precursors of pan-Africanism were numerous. Toussaint L'Ouverture, hero of the Haitian independence in 1791, remained a source of inspiration for all the blacks of the diaspora who were hostile to slavery. Paul Cuffee, a ship-owner from near Boston, Massachusetts, made his mission to develop commerce with black Africa in the 1830s. Along with Bishop Henry McNeal Turner, Doctor Martin Delany, graduate of Harvard University, defended the return of blacks to their native land in Africa and led an expedition to the Niger River basin in 1858. Alexander Crummell, native of New York and graduate of the University of Cambridge in England, was a minister in Liberia from 1853 to 1873 and a defender of black nationalism, despites his critique of certain archaic aspects of Africa.

To continue the list, the historian George Washington Williams defended the teaching of African history. Edward Blyden, originally from the island of Saint Thomas, who taught in Liberia and Sierra Leone from 1860 to 1890, was very impressed by the civilizations of the Futa Jallon and Kankan-Bate in Guinea. All these men criticized

European expansionism and contributed to the blossoming of pan-Africanism.

A new idea seems to have emerged from this earliest current of pan-Africanism. For these first theorists, the black world had encountered the most difficult and degrading period of its history in the nineteenth century. Despite the energetic leaps here and there, they reasoned, the African continent had difficulty re-establishing itself and creating viable institutions after the blood loss of the slave trade. Moreover, they added, the slave trade did not disappear right away despite its official abolition. Worse still, they observed, the powers that most benefited from the commercial slave trade began forcibly to occupy the interior of the continent. African kingdoms were not able to resist them effectively because of a lack of unity, but mostly because of a lack of modern armaments.

In the New World slavery thrived everywhere except for Haiti. Servitude was so rooted in the United States (where nevertheless black regiments had fought alongside the revolutionaries against England) that a long civil war was fought between 1861 and 1865 to stop the shame of bondage. But, as Nkrumah saw, slavery had been followed by the institution of repressive measures known as the "Jim Crow Law." This system of segregation and discrimination affected blacks in all aspect of their lives until the middle of the twentieth century.

In Cuba and Brazil, the emancipation of blacks was declared only in 1886 and 1888 respectively. Though free, members of these black communities remained at the bottom of society: poor, uneducated, and having little possibility for social advancement. The situation was no better in the old Spanish colonies of Latin America or in the Caribbean islands under French, English and Dutch control. The humiliation of the black race called for a cultural revolution and a great movement of solidarity and salvation. Pan-Africanism was linked to this imperative.

To corroborate this point of view, one can mention, for instance, the cooperation during the 1890s between black American churches and churches of South Africa and Nyasaland (Malawi). Indeed, the large black American congregation, called the African Methodist

Episcopal Church (AMEC), helped Christians in Africa to break with British and Swiss churches and to create their own institutions. Thus, on the two sides of the Atlantic, black communities, moved by the same inspiration, made religion a political ideology. It was the period of so-called "Ethiopian" churches because the term "Ethiopia" referred in Greek, just like the word "Sudan" in Arabic, to the region of black people.

With this movement of religious independence, the Christians of southern Africa embarked on a path of protesting and making demands. They demanded equality, stated the motto "Africa for Africans" and demanded a radical division of resources to allow Africans to flourish. Clearly, they were entering the area of politics. Many South African students received scholarships in black universities and seminaries in the United States. This is the origin of the education of several members of the black elite that would create the South African Native National Congress, precursor to the African National Congress (ANC). As it happens, Kwame Nkrumah benefited from such a scholarship to Lincoln University in 1935. This was an important stage in the development of pan-Africanism.

TWO GREAT PAN-AFRICANS

Nkrumah remembered two leaders: Edward Blyden and W. E. B. Du Bois. Their journey illustrated the depth of the pan-African dream. Born of free and literate parents in a multiracial and cosmopolitan quarter in St. Thomas in the Caribbean in 1832, Blyden received a good education. Very early on, he began to refer to his color as "ebony wood," which his parents attributed proudly to their Igbo origin. In 1842, after a long stay in Venezuela, he wondered why blacks always occupied the bottom of the ladder everywhere in the New World. Upon his return, in response to the call of his faith, he applied to a seminary in the United States. Because of his color, he was rejected. That was a shock.

Meanwhile, Blyden heard about the activities of the American Colonization Society, which supported the return of blacks to Africa.

Without hesitating or doubting the organization's motives, he decided to emigrate. And so, he arrived in Monrovia in January of 1851where he became the editor of a newspaper. He went on to enter the clergy and eventually became the principal of a college. His career notwithstanding, Blyden took a stand against the prejudice directed towards indigenous peoples from both mixed-race peoples and the Americo-Liberians. From 1862 to 1884, he served as a professor, diplomat, minister of foreign affairs and rector of the university. His reputation spread across the entire western coast of Africa under the increasing influence of England. He was the first to envision the idea of a united federation of states in West Africa.

Blyden was very interested in the history of domestic commerce and the role of Islam. In 1887, he abandoned Christianity for what he designated as "the religion of truth," and published a large work, *Christianity, Islam and the Negro Race*. Without being anti-Christian, this book presents Islam as a religion that is much more compatible with African civilizations. For him, Islam did not alienate blacks, as he observed at Timbo, Futa Jallon and Kankan in upper Guinea. Hollis R. Lynch rightly presented Blyden as "one of the great sons of Africa, the pioneer of pan-Africanism and negritude, the apostle of cooperation between the blacks of the two shores of the Atlantic."[23] He left an impact on the African elite and especially on the lieutenant-colonel doctor, Africanus Horton. Originally from Freetown and connected to the Turpin families of Saint-Louis in Senegal, Horton published numerous works on the need for developing superior technical education and for establishing unity in West Africa.

W. E. B. Du Bois is one of the great pan-Africanists. Dr. Martin Luther King, Jr. presented him as the one who attained the pinnacle of the moral and intellectual qualities on which the peoples of the black world prided themselves.[24] Born in 1868 near Boston, he was aware of racism from an early age, and resolved to combat it. He dedicated himself to his studies. At Harvard University, he pretended to overlook the segregation that he suffered. Du Bois always held a great interest in African affairs. He wondered, for instance, about the Congress of Berlin and events in the Congo, Anglo-Egyptian Sudan, and southern Africa. His experience as a student in Berlin helped him to better appreciate the extent of racism in European culture and to deepen his knowledge of modern philosophy and emerging social sciences. He decided then to put his knowledge in service to the struggle against racist ideology.

Kwame Nkrumah, W. E. B. Du Bois and Shirley Graham Du Bois.

Back in the United States, Du Bois taught for a long time at Atlanta University, where he forcefully oriented social sciences to the study of racial questions. He impressed everyone by his capacity to think as a man of action and to act as a man of thought. With Jews and other liberal whites, he created the National Association for the Advancement of Colored People (NAACP) in 1889. This organization distinguished itself by the litigation it brought against racist practices throughout the United States. By necessity, this anti-racist struggle turned towards Africa. Du Bois entered the movement of pan-Africanism and assumed its direction. Here is how he explained his fervor:

> What is Africa to me…. What is it between us that constitutes a tie, which I can feel better than I can explain? Africa is, of course, my fatherland. Yet neither my father nor my father's father ever saw Africa or knew its meaning or cared overmuch for it…. still, my tie to Africa is strong. On this vast continent were born and lived a large portion of my direct ancestor…. The mark of their heritage is upon me in color and hair. These are obvious things, but of little meaning in themselves…. the real essence of this kinship is its social heritage of slavery; the discrimination and insult…. It is this unity that draws me to Africa.[25]

In addition to emotion, Du Bois brought to pan-Africanism a rational justification based on historical and sociological facts. In an article published in 1919, he compared pan-Africanism to Zionism in these terms: "The African movement means to us what the Zionist movement must mean to the Jews, the centralization of race effort and the recognition of a racial fount."[26] To reinforce this idea, he went to Africa in 1929 and immersed himself in African life before beginning to organize the pan-African congresses. It was later at one these conferences in Manchester where the student Nkrumah made his acquaintance in 1945.

PAN-AFRICAN CONGRESSES AND THE DREAM OF UNITY, 1900–1945

During the crossing, Nkrumah did not stop thinking about pan-Africanism. This movement was, at the outset, an American manifestation and impulse. From 1900 to 1945, blacks of the diaspora dominated the movement, and Du Bois institutionalized it. In his work, *Pan-Africanism or Communism*, Trinidadian journalist George Padmore neglected to speak of the London conference in 1900. And yet, his compatriot, the lawyer H. Sylvester Williams, known for his pan-Africanist ideas, was its principal organizer. How can this silence be explained? Whatever the case, this meeting deserves to be considered the first pan-African congress.

A great many members of the black American clergy attended the congress at Westminster Hall from July 23-25, 1900. One of Sylvester Williams' collaborators, Bishop Alexander Walters of the

AMEC, presided over the sessions. The conference centered on the topics of religion and politics. Among the 32 delegates there were four representatives from Africa: the aide-de-camp of Emperor Menelik II of Ethiopia, the former guardian of the seals of Liberia, a territorial adviser from Sierra Leone and a lawyer from the Gold Coast. There were also 11 delegates from the USA and 13 from the Caribbean.

After the welcome address of the Bishop of London, discussions focused on the conditions of black people. In this time of war between the English and Afrikaners, the speakers remarked with regret on the ambiguity of British policy towards Africans, as well as the intensification of racism in South Africa. They addressed a message to Queen Victoria inviting her to remedy this policy.[27]

Du Bois was responsible for addressing a message to all nations of the world on behalf of the conference. With a prophetic tongue, he predicted that the crucial problem of the twentieth century is the problem of color and race, that is, the relations between peoples of white race and those of dark race.[28] For the millions of black people in the world, he demanded justice and freedom. He reminded European powers of the need to respect the independence of Ethiopia, Liberia, and Haiti. The discussions were a testimony to their consciousness of unity.

People's support for pan-Africanism remained a problem for a long time. As an example, Colin Legum accused Du Bois of being "'tiresomely proud of his own Dutch and French ancestors.... a vain, prickly, egocentric intellectual."[29] This virulent judgment manifestly lacks rock-solid foundation. Du Bois excelled in his work as an engaged intellectual. But another individual, Marcus Garvey, would play the leading role in the emerging popular pan-African current.

Born in Jamaica, Marcus Garvey immigrated to New York where he organized a mass movement. Owing to his sense of organization, all black America, from urban ghettos to rural towns in the South, from chapels to amphitheaters, became aware of Africa and of the positive signification of black skin. His influence reached West and central Africa as well as African communities in Europe.

Temperamentally different, Du Bois and Garvey came into opposition very early. Du Bois, an activist intellectual accustomed to cold analyses and measured expressions, made an impression through his aristocratic aspect. Garvey, short and stocky, "with eyes full of malice," was an exuberant chief, interesting and interested, who knew how to move the masses through his well-made formulas and his sense of comedy that his detractors took for farce. Garvey's stances were often unpredictable and controversial (for example, his alliance with the chiefs of the negrophobic organization, the Ku Klux Klan). Impulsive and abrasive in his speech, he incurred the hostility of the black elite whom he ridiculed because its members were not all pure black blood. It is a tragedy that there was an opposition between these two leaders. Yet Garvey's movement did not contradict Du Bois's great pan-Africanist views. Both movements promoted unity and respect for black people everywhere in the world.

As for Nkrumah, he presently continued his reflection on the pan-African congresses. Given the scope of the Great War ending in 1918, Du Bois considered it necessary to hold a conference in Paris, where the Allies would discuss the terms of peace. The task was far from easy.

The colonial powers and American government refused to grant passports or visas to blacks considered to be "militant." But Du Bois succeeded in maneuvering around it, thanks to the help of Madame Calman-Levy and especially Blaise Diagne, elected member of the French National Assembly (deputy) from Senegal and a high official in the War Ministry responsible for the recruitment of black soldiers. Coming from Diagne, whose attitudes were contradictory to Du Bois's as Amady Aly Dieng has shown, this seemed strange.[30] In this way, Du Bois received authorization from Clemenceau, the head of the French government, to hold the congress.

The second pan-African congress took place at the Grand Hotel July 19-21, 1919 with the participation of twelve delegates from nine African countries.[31] Most of these delegates were in Paris because of the war and for other reasons. The group of African nationalists in Paris, including Lamine Senghor from Senegal, Garan Kouyaté of

French Sudan (Mali) and others, attended. With some forty delegates, however, the diaspora was still dominant.

The resolutions did not yet demand the colonies' right to independence. They asked instead for a code of laws and an international office for the protection of black people, the participation of colonial subjects in the affairs of their countries, and the right to education. The congress delegates questioned the transfer of German colonies as mandates to other powers and opposed South Africa's stranglehold on the former German territory of southwest Africa (Namibia).

Considering the complexity of the problems that arose after 1918, Du Bois thought that the movement must hold regular meetings. Thus, the third pan-African congress took place in summer 1921, and due to opposition from authorities, it was first in London from August 28-29, then in Brussels from August 31 to September 2, and finally in Paris on September 4. Pan-Africanism had become synonymous with anti-colonialism and in European capitals some thought that the Bolsheviks, who had just succeeded in their revolution in Russia, supported the movement.[32]

There were many African and American delegates. In contrast, Caribbean participation was weak, probably because of the opposition between Garvey and Du Bois. In London, the delegates denounced Belgium's colonial policy, but in Brussels Blaise Diagne managed to moderate the tone. In the final report, published in Paris, the conference described racism as "the most stupid form of the social divisions" and invited governments to work toward suppressing it.

Because of the new international context, the congress delegates gave Du Bois the task of presenting their grievances at the League of Nations in Geneva. Discussions there were fruitful, despite the opposition of American observers disgruntled by criticism of their intervention in Haiti in 1916. The petition written by Du Bois against South African policy was published as an official document of the League of Nations. The fourth congress convened in 1926, first in London, then in Lisbon. The South African situation was still a cause for concern.

Most pan-Africanists attended the League's meeting against imperialism in Brussels in February 1927. The first of its type, this conference showed the international dimension in the struggle against racism. Garan Kouyaté; Lamine Senghor; the vice-president of the ANC, J. T. Gumedé; and the South African writer, J. A. La Guma, presented the African dossier to the conference attendants, among whom were Sukarno (the future president of Indonesia) and Nehru (the future prime minister of India). This anti-imperialist congress was the prelude to the conference of non-allied countries at Bandung in 1955.

The fifth conference was held in New York from August 21-24, 1927, under Du Bois's presidency. There were more than 200 delegates, including those from the Gold Coast, Nigeria, and Sierra Leone. This was the time of internationalism.

The slogan "Africa for Africans" was launched, and the exploitation of African wealth by foreigners was condemned. The congress delegates also denounced the United States' policy in Central America and expressed their gratitude to the Soviet Union for its support of anti-colonialist movements. A resolution very much in agreement with the spirit of pan-Africanism called for Caribbean leaders to form a federation of islands to ensure their development. From this point on, pan-Africanism claimed to be political and militant. This orientation suited the international context that emerged in 1945.

NKRUMAH AND THE CONGRESS AT MANCHESTER

The traveler Nkrumah thus landed at Liverpool after five days of fruitful reflection aboard the ship. He knew no one in England, except by name the journalist George Padmore, to whom he had written to announce his arrival. To his great surprise Padmore was waiting for him at the train station platform in London. A current passed naturally between them, and it was the beginning of a long friendship.

Padmore obtained accommodations for him at the residence for West African students and introduced him to London's black community. Nkrumah quickly felt confined and ill-at-ease in the academic residence with its strict visiting hours and snobbish atmosphere. In looking for new accommodations, he was fortunate to run into his compatriot, Ako Adjei, whom he had not seen since the United States years ago. Together they set themselves on the hunt for student rooms, a very difficult experience for non-white people. At last, they found "digs" at 60 Burghley Road in a working neighborhood at the house of simple, kind and generous family. Exceedingly humble in turn, Nkrumah was not reluctant to do laundry for the couple, work habit that helped him earn a little extra money in difficult months as a poor student in Philadelphia. He would spend his entire visit there from June 1945 to November 1947.[33]

Nkrumah's residence at 60 Burghley Road in Kentish Town, London.

Kwame Nkrumah wanted to study law and to finish his doctorate in philosophy, and so he enrolled at the university. However, he rapidly found himself fully involved in political activism. As in the United States, he made contact with many schools of thought, including the communist party. He joined the West African Students' Union and helped Africans who had just arrived to find lodging, to enroll at the university, and to resolve other problems. These were the circumstances in which he became Padmore's indispensable aid for organizing the pan-African conference at Manchester in October 1945. This was the sixth congress.

The organizing committee named Nkrumah and Padmore as secretaries. Morning and evening, with the British Guiana (Guyana) born and naturalized Kenyan citizen T. R. Makonnen, the South African novelist Peter Abrahams and Professor C. L. R. James, they worked on correspondence, reserving hotel rooms, and creating a coherent program and other activities necessary for the conference's success. As expected, the congress opened under the presidency of Du Bois.

For the first-time students, workers and common people attended the sessions *en masse*. Besides delegates from the Caribbean, Europe and North America, there were also representatives from India, Ceylon (Sri Lanka) and Cyprus. With over twenty-six participants, black Africa increasingly assumed control of the pan-African movement.

In addition to Peter Abrahams, Makonnen, and Nkrumah, it is important to note the presence of S. L. Akintola and Awolowo, both future political leaders of Nigeria, the Togolese poet Raphael Armattoé, Jomo Kenyatta, Wallace Johnson of Sierra Leone, the historian J. C. de Graft Johnson of the Gold Coast, Dr. Hastings Banda, future president of Nyasaland, and others still who would contribute to the political awakening of their respective countries.

*President Jomo Kenyatta of Kenya and President Kwame
Nkrumah of Ghana, ca. 1965.*

The congress paid lively homage to the septuagenarian W. E. B.
Du Bois for his work in the service of the movement. Henceforth,
he would hold the title of "father of pan-Africanism." Along with
Nkrumah, he was made responsible for writing up the official declaration addressing the "imperialist powers." In this document the
conference members asserted "the determination of the colonized
peoples to obtain their freedom," and condemned "the monopoly
of private capital and the use of wealth for personal ends." The resolutions focused on the imperative of realizing the slogan "Africa
for Africans"; the need to create the United States of Africa and to
develop nationalism instead of tribalism; and the necessity of universal suffrage based on "one person, one vote" in southern Africa.
Nkrumah was delighted that the congress adopted socialism as its
philosophy.[34]

The Manchester conference was different from the preceding
ones. The large participation of Africans steered the debates toward

the critical issues of the hour, such as the crisis of colonialism and the rise of nationalism. The discussions then centered on resolving concrete problems. According to Nkrumah, Africans adopted pan-African nationalism to awaken the popular conscience and to create a mass movement with a view to independence.[35]

Immediately after Manchester, Nkrumah and other activists created a supra-territorial, West African movement under Du Bois's presidency, whose mission was to support self-determination everywhere. Nkrumah was named secretary general. He worked tirelessly during these months. In contact with numerous union and political organizations, he became one of the best-known young leaders.

The plan of holding a West African conference in Lagos, Nigeria in October 1948 brought him to Paris, where he encountered the African elected representatives to the French National Assembly Lamine Guèye, Leopold Senghor, Souru Apithy, Houphouët-Boigny and others. He organized a conference in London, where Senghor and Apithy spoke in favor of West African unity. The dream of a regional unity beyond colonial borders was being outlined.

For the first time, Nkrumah began to think that perhaps Africans could accomplish what the American revolutionaries of 1776 had achieved. Time, however, would show if his dream would materialize. Meanwhile, an unexpected opportunity would change his immediate plans, and it appeared a prodigious project that could promote the spirit of the Manchester conference.

3

THE INDEPENDENCE OF GHANA AND PLANNING THE DREAM

The Manchester conference made Kwame Nkrumah popular in Anglophone Africa. In his birth country itself, he became known to members of the urban elite, who were commonly called "the haves." The people of little means, called "veranda boys," who knew how to read, respected him for his unambiguous attitudes. They thought he might be able to play a role in the Gold Coast.

In England, the black community appreciated Nkrumah for his activism and his simplicity. He served as arbiter between African students and workers, who were already numerous in the large cities. To continue the work of the congress, he set up within the student association a frontline organization called "Circle," whose members were trained in the practices of political unrest, aimed at the struggle for decolonization and unity.

But Kwame did not forget the Gold Coast. It was his country and, as he contemplated, the point of departure for a political movement bound to actualize the grand ideals from Manchester. He dreamed of returning. Truth be told, he was homesick, for he had left twelve years earlier. Alas, the country was far and he was as poor as a church mouse. A good African citizen, he often thought about the blessings of his parents and about God, as Azikiwe had suggested to him. As though by miracle, something unexpected happened.

RETURN TO HIS COUNTRY

One day Nkrumah received a letter from Ako Adjei, an old acquaintance he had known in London, who had returned to Accra. On behalf of a group of "important people" commonly called "the haves," Adjei invited him to take up the duties as secretary general of a political movement known as "The United Gold Coast Convention" (UGCC). They offered him a monthly salary of 100 sterling pounds (around 400 dollars) and a company vehicle—a staggering remuneration for the time. This organization, perhaps the most important in the country, was in crisis.

The problem it faced was how to keep its character as an elite movement and at the same time attract the popular masses. The "haves" represented both the traditional aristocracy and the new urban upper bourgeoisie. In an oligarchical spirit, the UGCC had been founded in August 1947 by a group of academics, wealthy shopkeepers, planters, and leaders. But none of them were ready to give up a lucrative career to dedicate himself to the task of organizing.

These oligarchs knew that they needed the people's support to legitimize their position, to obtain concessions from the colonial governor and to guide the country in this period of change. Without publicly admitting so, they thought that a villager of humble origin, who held university diplomas and demonstrated his aptitude as an organizer, could "do the trick." This explains why the invitation was issued to Nkrumah, and highlights the existing social division.[36]

Nkrumah considered the offer. The money interested him less than the post. He thought about the possibilities afforded by the secretariat of an organization with branches in all regions of the country. Was this not an exceptional opportunity for him as an activist? But the details that he obtained about the UGCC hardly reassured him. The Union was conservative, and its leaders were arrogant and narrow-minded. He gave up the idea. But a second letter arrived. Sent by Dr. J. B. Danquah, the principal leader of the UGCC, it begged Nkrumah to accept the offer and to come without delay. Kwame reflected and decided to try his luck.

On the November 4, 1947, Nkrumah and his comrade Kojo Bot-sio, treasurer of the students' association, left London for Liverpool. Before leaving, Kwame was interrogated for a long time by security services concerning his affiliation with the communist party. In Free-town, he gave lectures and had discussions with the trade unionist Wallace Johnson and other nationalists. In Monrovia, he saw what could go wrong in an independent black state. Then in December, amid ordinary people on deck of a boat, he arrived in Takoradi, the sole port of the Gold Coast at the time. He landed incognito to avoid the police.[37]

Without wasting time, he headed to the home of his friend Ack-wa Watson in Tarkwa, where his mother Nyaniba was waiting for him. The encounter of mother and son was a shock at first. They had both changed a lot since 1935. The son was surprised to see the toll that time had taken on his mother over the last twelve years. She had become frail and her vision was weak. Like all children, he had thought her eternally vigorous and beautiful.

As for Nyaniba she had trouble recognizing her son Kwame. The teeth that were unique to him were no longer the same! Was some-one playing a trick on her? To reassure herself, she used her sense of touch, took his hand, and examined the fingers that were peculiar to him. Their familiar thickness finally revealed to her the identity of her only son. The tears began to pour. She thanked God for this memorable day. Mother and son gazed at one another. They were happy. They spent two joyful weeks together. Kwame rested, recov-ered his strength, and considered conditions in the Gold Coast.

THE GOLD COAST IN 1947

The Gold Coast had changed since 1935. There was an appearance of growth, affluence, and social transformation despite the trials of war. The authorities gladly considered this country "the model colony par excellence." It was calm, peaceful, prosperous, and re-spectful of power. In everyone's mind, it was a territory that would soon be called to exercise its political autonomy within the context of an intelligent constitutional reform and, better, under the auspices of its legitimate chiefs who were all known for their political moderation. The indigenous masses were described as serious workers and as loyal subjects to their chiefs. It appeared to be a territory without problems, for which the colonial administration congratulated itself. Such was the fantasy image of the world where Kwame Nkrumah had just landed. But does the image correspond to reality? The new arrival asked himself this question.

Unlike Gambia, Sierra Leone or even its neighbors under French colonial rule, the Gold Coast had numerous assets. The country was relatively large, populated and effectively governed. The resources were numerous and quite diverse. It was an important colony with a population of nearly five million inhabitants. Unlike the other territories of West Africa, including Nigeria, ethnic diversity was not a great factor here.

Indeed, the great majority of the population belonged to the same Akan stock and spoke languages that were related to or variations of the same language. Asante or Twi lived in the center around Kumasi; Brong (Bono) were in the chiefdoms of the west; Akuapem-Twi in the hill region behind Accra; Fante on the coast to the west of Accra; Gá in Accra itself; and Ewe to the east of the Volta.

Culturally, only the less populous and developed Northern region was different, and its languages—Dagomba, Gonja, Farefare and Samo—belonged to the Voltaic or Mandinka branch. The extension of the cocoa culture, a main source of prosperity, made the linguistic and demographic profile even more complex with the migration of a large population of Mossi, Zarma and Hausa.

Urbanization had made progress. In 1947, Accra and Kumase were the two largest cities with 150,000 and 80,000 inhabitants respectively. Sekondi-Takoradi, Cape Coast, and Tamale in the north became important urban zones, with running water, electricity, and roads that were shaded and paved. However, the urban population was small compared to the rural population. As a sign of social diversification, it counted over 200,000 people involved in cocoa production, nearly 40,000 workers in gold or bauxite mines, and nearly 30,000 in municipal services.[38]

The regions were linked to one another by a rail and road system, generally well maintained and comprised of more than 1,000 kilometers of paved roads. People traveled a lot. Local and regional markets saw a great deal of activity owing to exchanges between shopkeepers and farmers. At this level, one observed the increasingly important role of women in specialized commerce. The foreign trade balance and territorial budget were in surplus.

The culture and commerce of cocoa were key revenue sources. These agricultural activities gave rise to a prosperous and active African rural and urban bourgeoisie, whose children, ever increasing in number, studied in England, and later entered various professions. It was the origin of a new class, called "the intellectuals." They were university graduates, differed from those who only completed primary studies, and belonged to the elite. From their offices as lawyers, doctors, and accountants, they were very active on the urban stage, they were wealthy and sure of themselves; moreover, they maintained close ties to the chiefs. This explains, in part, the source of the Gold Coast's advantage over other territories. This report, positive in superficial ways, hardly impressed Nkrumah. An authentic son of Nkroful, a village in a well-watered region, he had learned to distrust still water. He would not hesitate to try and explore the depths of the well or river.

Wealth and education, as with birth and power, had become the criteria for social differentiation. A triumvirate comprised of the governor, chiefs and intellectuals possessed most of the power, and tried to perpetuate their domination despite their differences. Nkrumah examined the social effect of capitalism and the question of class in African society. He concluded that political action had to focus on the way poor people could become a dynamic force and overthrow the social balance. Thus, he assigned great importance to education.

The preceding observations brought Nkrumah back to his childhood in the village. Born on a Saturday, at his baptism he received the name of Kwame, as was customary in the Akan world. His father had been a blacksmith, strong of character and generous (in contrast with the civilizations of the savannah, blacksmiths did not form a caste among the Akan). His mother, who was very religious, had him baptized at the local Catholic Church by the German priest George Fischer. Fischer recorded his birth date as September 21, 1909, and he left a deep imprint on Nkrumah.

By virtue of the matrilineal system, Nkrumah could lay claim through his mother to two chiefdoms in the north of Nzema. Nevertheless, he knew that his family was poor. For this reason, many communities, like his own, considered schooling important because it could positively enhance the social condition of graduates. In 1947, the enrollment rate reached thirty percent in the country, a sign of remarkable advancement.

After eight years in school, Nkrumah was a teaching instructor at Half-Assini, a small town not far from Nkroful. His ability so impressed the regional superintendent of schools that he was able to enter the teachers' college of Achimota and graduate as a licensed teacher. In the top of his class, he taught along the coast at Elmina, Axim, and the small seminary of Amissano. He avidly read the writings of Nnamdi Azikiwe and Wallace Johnson, which gave him the courage to undertake his education in the United States.

Returned now to his homeland, Nkrumah attached even more importance to schooling and to the graduates of primary and secondary schools. He was familiar with this group and the conditions in which its members lived. He understood their problems and aspirations, and better still, he had an idea of the role that they could play in nationalism. As educators, court clerks, higher civil servants, junior officers, accountants, storekeepers, leaders of union offices, even the unemployed, they will represent a real force, when and if they are mobilized. They were the catalysts of anticolonial sentiment. Hence, the intellectuals and chiefs who formed the group of the "haves" wanted to forge links with them in order to control them.

But the interests of the "haves" and those of primary school graduates diverged. The latter were wage earners: poorly paid, without the right to strike, without social advantages; they were disrespected, and were therefore discontent. Their plight gives an objective glimpse of conditions for much of the urban city dwellers. These literate individuals of the lower echelon wanted a radical change instead of the mild reforms that satisfied the elite. They were not revolutionaries, but they could assume the role of organizers and frontline activists once they became aware of themselves and their strength. In sum, in the eyes of Nkrumah, the Gold Coast was far from being "a model colony." Rather, it was powder keg that could explode in an unexpected way.

The colonial administration, directed by the governor and his cabinet, aimed to control, if not slow down, this process of radical transformation. In 1947, the high administration remained a domain reserved for British expatriates. These civil servants lived far from the indigenous peoples in their own neighborhoods such as Cantonments, Ridge, and Christiansborg in Accra. These neighborhoods were foreign to Nkrumah. This system of segregation corresponded to the Manichean universe which Frantz Fanon spoke about in his analysis of the colonial world.[39] This is a world cut into two conflicting parts, one unclean, hungry, infected, filthy, poorly lit and ill-paved for the natives, and the other well-kept and well-fed for the European colonizers.

The central government communicated with the popular masses through their intermediary officials, the chiefs. Logically, conquest by Europeans led to the suppression of precolonial Africa political authority. Defeated, exiled, or deposed, the leaders, regardless of their names, lost their power. As in the Asante kingdom, their territories were divided and granted to new dignitaries named by the colonial administration according to their own criteria. These observations apply to the so-called regime of "direct administration" in force in the French colonies as well as to the regime of "indirect administration" applied in certain English territories. At the level of structure and function, chiefdoms ceased to be "traditional" and became a constitutive element of the new colonial political order.

Nkrumah thought that this change in legitimacy transformed the status of chiefs in relation to their subjects. In reality, the traditional chiefs, whatever their title, no longer represented their subjects. They were responsible to the colonial administration that named them. Consequently, they were genuine agents of the colonial system, and as such, they formed part of the apparatus of domination despite their origin and color.

Unlike the French colonial regime, however, the chiefdom on the Gold Coast was made up of important offices. For example, the *Asantehene* (ruler) of the Asante possessed prerogatives far superior to those of the *Mogho-naba* (King of the Mossi) at Ouagadougou in Burkina Faso, of the *Almami* (Muslim ruler) in Futa Jallon, or of the *Kanda* (village leader) at Kankan-Baté in Guinea. Besides their apparent wealth, the traditional chiefs of the Gold Coast directed true administrative units, with specialized services and control over primary education, land ownership, and civil law. Moreover, as presidents of regional assemblies they were represented in the governor's executive council. Their influence had even increased since the early 1940s, when Governor Burns, considered an enlightened administrator, introduced reforms.[40]

With Burns' reforms, black civil servants were named assistant "circle commanders." Africans could vote in municipal elections. The constitution of 1946 enlarged the number of members of the governor's executive council and reinforced the position of the chiefs within this organization. The latter were also responsible for the elaboration of development programs. The administration wanted to make the chiefdom a modern institution capable of managing the country after decolonization.

In 1947, the aristocratic families enjoyed another political trump due to their family members who belonged to the group of intellectuals and "haves." For instance, J. B. Danquah, Kofi Busia, Ako Adjei, Simon Dombo and Joe Appiah were all of princely origins.[41] Governor Burns' reforms aimed not only at any radical nationalist unrest but also at preparing for the transfer of power to the "haves." Indeed, Burns received the support of Danquah, who invited Nkrumah to return, and who was the brother of Nana Ofori Atta, famous king of the Akyem, in the south of Kumase. At Tarkwa, near his mother's home, Nkrumah concluded that the chiefs represented the conservative element, both powerful and firmly rooted.

Taking this view of the whole, Kwame Nkrumah seemed to understand his country better. In addition to the contrast between urban and rural sectors or between Christian and Muslim, there was an even stronger opposition between the power holders and the subjects, or in a word, between the people and the elite. A champion of pan-Africanism, Nkrumah dreamed of uniting all these layers within a great movement. It remained to be known whether the UGCC could open itself to the entire world. That was the challenge. And Nkrumah was already beginning a program aimed at making the UGCC the lead organization in the struggle for self-determination. But would they give him free reign?

Before leaving his mother and beginning his work at the office of the UGCC at Saltpond on the coast, he held his first public meeting at the school of Tarkwa, where he noted with pleasure the presence of miners and of other workers. In a speech using both English and indigenous languages, he spoke of his experience abroad and presented his vision for the country's future. He received the audience's ovation. As though charmed, the people were ready to fight for social progress. This first experience amid the crowd gave him hope, and he got back to his work at Saltpond.

SETTING THE FIRE: THE CREATION OF THE PARTY

Nkrumah was enthusiastically received by the members of the UGCC's general staff. The issue of his nomination arose in the agenda at this first meeting. He soon realized that the salary that was proposed to him was only bait, since the organization lacked funds because of its political activities.

To everyone's disbelief, Nkrumah declared that he was prepared to work without a salary, if his lodging and other expenses were guaranteed. "Bizarre, bizarre," they thought. "He's either stupid or he has an ulterior motive." Finally, they offered him twenty-five pounds sterling, and he accepted. The members of the executive committee informed him of their intention to work for the abolition of the Burns constitution, but without being more specific. He set up his office.

On January 20, 1948, Nkrumah submitted a concrete plan for the movement's success to the executive committee. His plan saw the need for master coordination of the various organizations affiliated with the UGCC, the need to create activist cells everywhere and to improve the political formation of members, and proposed a national conference on the question of autonomy. Strikes, rallies, and boycotts on stores and services seemed necessary. However, in the discussions, he realized that the leaders of the UGCC were not interested in the entire Gold Coast, but only in the coastal zone and the Asante at the center. Moreover, only two branches of the association were operating.

Meanwhile, the riots of February and March 1948 broke out. They were due to the protests of Nii Kwabena Bonne, chief of a district in the region of Accra and critic of the high cost of living, and they were also linked to the demands of former combatants returning from Burma (Myanmar) and the Middle East. Nkrumah was not associated with these movements when he held his first meeting at the Palladium cinema, in Accra on February 28, 1948.

Speaking as a former student, Nkrumah addressed the members of the league of young students about the "Ideological Battles of Our Time." Despite its title, this speech was not abstract. Very simply, the speaker reminded the young of their duty toward the Gold Coast and all western Africa. He urged them to excel in their studies to assume political responsibilities. Like the crowd's reaction at Tarkwa, the reaction here at Accra confirmed the readiness of the "Ghanaians," a term already in use by Nkrumah and other leaders.

On this same day, February 28, coinciding with the end of the store boycotts, veterans demonstrated in the administrative quarter. As they approached the governor's residence at Christiansborg Castle, the police ordered the demonstrators to stop. They refused. In response, the English police officer ordered his men to shoot. Two former soldiers, Sergeants Adjetey and Attipoe, fell dead on the spot, and several others were wounded. Like a spark, the news lit fires as it spread. All whites, English, Lebanese and even Indian people were under attack, as were department stores and administrative offices. The riot lasted several days. The governor declared a state of emergency. Twenty-nine people were killed and 237 were injured. This unexpected situation would change many things.

On his return to Saltpond, Nkrumah called an urgent meeting of the leaders of the UGCC. They decided that they had to bring the events to the knowledge of the Colonial Secretary in London. Two telegrams were sent, one in the name of the people, another in the name of the chiefs, demanding a special investigative commission. The UGCC's lease was annulled and Nkrumah had to move his offices to Cape Coast.

Governor Gerald Creasy gave the order to arrest Nkrumah and five members of the executive committee (Danquah, Ofori Atta, Akufo Addo, Ako Adjei, Obetsebi Lamptey). Together they were the "Big Six," historical prisoners of 1948. But, thrown together in the same cell, they revealed their differences. The others resented Nkrumah. They held him responsible for their misfortune and blamed Adjei for having proposed his name as secretary. They were all deported to the North, each to a different prison.

In April 1948, the prisoners were brought back to Accra before the arrival of the parliamentary commission presided over by Aiken Watson, the king's counselor. The prisoners were set free. The commission considered Nkrumah's experience in the United States and London. The documents seized in his room concerning "the Circle" and an unsigned British Communist Party Card raised suspicions. Danquah and the other leaders of the UGCC separated themselves from him.

In May 1948, the Watson commission published its report. It accused the members of the UGCC of taking advantage of Nkrumah's experience to "seize power at an opportune moment." Nkrumah was painted as a dangerous propagandist, capable of using "techniques of communist slavery" and of creating a "Union of African Soviet Socialist Republics." However, the Watson commission recommended that the British government "block" the Burns constitution, which "no longer corresponded to reality," and to introduce a new one written by Africans themselves.

In December 1948, Governor Creasy named a constitutional committee of forty members, including chiefs, intellectuals, rich businessmen and important civil servants. The African judge Henley Coussey was president of the commission. The union members, the middle classes and the workers were not represented.

Meanwhile, the leaders of the UGCC led their investigation into Nkrumah's political affiliation. They rebuked him for his speeches, his stances and his "fantasies." They could not believe that their general secretary founded newspapers without their knowledge.[42] Worse, they had trouble understanding why their employee used his own funds to support students and instructors fired after the demonstrations of March 1948. Not only did he pay for education, but he also supported all the staff in a new school called "Ghana College." For them, this was a sign of betrayal. They labeled Nkrumah a "communist" because he often used the word "comrade" in his correspondence and greetings! Finally, they asked for his resignation.

At this moment, the youth league of the UGCC, now active and counting many members, expressed its discontent with the Coussey Commission as well as with its leadership. Komla Gbedemah, Kojo Botsio, Kofi Baako and Saki Scheck appeared like the chiefs of these "young Turks," to use Padmore's expression .[43] They organized a national congress in December, while Nkrumah was visiting Côte d'Ivoire and Kankan in Guinea. The young people demanded a constitution from the Coussey Commission with the slogan "self-determination now." Thus, a crisis broke out between the leaders of the UGCC and its youth members.

Nkrumah nevertheless seemed to hesitate and look for a compromise. He did not wish to fragment the nascent national movement or to burn any bridges. He believed that the field of nationalism was sufficiently vast to allow the coexistence of different currents. He also feared the colonial administration's capacity to divide and rule. Pragmatically, he wished the directors of the UGCC would understand the needs of the time and collaborate with different segments of society based on an unambiguous nationalist program. Faced with the reluctance of "the old guard" and the Coussey Commission's refusal to consider the idea of immediate autonomy, the young members decided to break with the UGCC.

On Sunday, June 12, 1949, the youth league invited the people to an "extraordinary meeting" on the grounds of the market in the old neighborhood of Arena or London Market, whose former name goes back to the period of the slave trade. The crowd rushed from the four corners of the village and from the neighboring villages. The place was literally stormed by these men and women, all driven by their desire to participate in political life. This human tide of over 60,000 people stood as a single being, listening, awe-struck, to the analysis of recent events and the announcement of a new dawn.

In a strong and solemn voice, the speaker asked the crowd "must I leave the country as the bosses of the UGCC advised me?" The answer "NO, NO" resounded like thunder in the large square. A new question followed: "Must I immediately break off with the UGCC since it is not resolved to lead the fight?" The response was instantaneous. In unison, the crowd chanted, "YES, YES, IMMEDIATELY."

When calm was restored, Nkrumah thanked the audience and announced the league's decision to transform itself into a political party. As he later explained:

> Then, on behalf of the CYO in the name of the chiefs and the people, the rank and file of the Convention, the Labor Movement, our valiant ex-servicemen, the youth movement throughout the country, the man in the street, our children and those yet unborn, the new Ghana that is to be, Sergeant Adjetey and his comrades who died at the crossroads of Christiansborg during the riots of 12 June 1948, and in the name of God Almighty and humanity, I declared to the crowd the birth of the Convention People's Party (CPP) which would, from that day forward, carry on the struggle for the liberation of our dear Ghana in the recognized party system, until full self-government was won for the chiefs and people of the country.[44]

This action represents a remarkable evolution in the political history of the Gold Coast. Up until then, the people had expressed their discontent through individual coalitions or spontaneous demonstrations without a long-term program, structure, or precise ideology. Strictly speaking, the UGCC and similar organizations do not deserve the name of "parties," but rather of "movements" which rise and fall in the course of events. This was a shortcoming. Nkrumah knew that nationalism demanded a structured and effective political channel. The CPP established a new political dynamic in the Gold Coast and set an example for nationalists in British territories.

The composition of the party reflected the urban social division. At the start, the CPP was made up of an assembly of salaried workers who had decided to fight, spread their ideas, and mobilize the workers and farmers, hence the name "Convention." The party rejected tribalism, regionalism, and sectarianism.

The program focused on the following six points: 1) to fight for immediate autonomy; 2) to eliminate all forms of oppression and to establish a democratic government; 3) to reinforce unity between the chiefs and people; 4) to defend the interest of workers and the union movement; 5) to make the Gold Coast a state under the rule of law; and 6) to promote unity in west Africa by all means necessary. These ideas lead Nkrumah and his party to realize the other steps of their struggle.

INDEPENDENCE IN UNITY

Nkrumah and his supporters sprang into action. At Accra and on the coast, mobilization resulted in the creation of numerous branches in the space of a few weeks. With gifts and their collective funds, the party bought vans on which they attached loudspeakers to spread their message. The CPP became a force everywhere, including the central and northern territories. The opposition did not remain inactive either. It led a campaign against the "communists," the "gangsters," the "veranda boys" and the "foreigners" who "sowed mayhem" in "the Ga country" (a reference to Nkrumah who was not from Accra, a city situated in the heart of the region where the Ga language was prevalent).

The CPP had already distinguished itself by its stances on the emancipation of women, who suffered twofold for their color and their gender. Thus, women of all means responded favorably to its message. They became deeply involved in political action. As

Nkrumah noted in his autobiography, vegetable sellers, cloth sellers and simple housewives made themselves available to the party as information secretaries and standard-bearers for solidarity and unity. Thus, the party became a national movement that clearly expressed the people's hopes. In the space of two months, Nkrumah's image had become that of a charismatic leader.

Two months after the CPP's creation, the Coussey Commission published its report on the plans for a new constitution. The governor C. Arden-Clarke, who had replaced Creasy, quickly promulgated the new constitution. It proposed to establish a semi-autonomous system of government. An executive counsel consisting of three *ex-officio* members and eight appointed ministers was responsible for the government.[45] An assembly of 75 members, of whom two-thirds were elected by the taxpayers and the other third chosen by the council of chiefs, decided the laws. This constitution was neither revolutionary nor democratic. It corresponded to the views of the UGCC and chiefs.

The CPP's reaction was not long coming. Nkrumah unequivocally rejected the constitution since it ignored the principles of democracy and autonomy. His party promised to lead a "positive action," which is to say, a campaign of strikes and other public demonstrations to achieve the necessary reforms. In other words, Nkrumah envisaged a non-violent campaign based on the idea of civil disobedience in the manner of Mahatma Gandhi in India.

To strengthen its position, the CPP held a massive conference on November 20 in Accra. Literally the first of its kind in the country, it aimed at cohesion and unity in opposition to the administration. With the participation of over fifty organizations, Nkrumah did not hesitate to call it "the Constitutive Assembly of Representatives of the People of Ghana." Delegates came from everywhere and from all social levels, except for the chiefs, the Aborigines' Rights Protection Society and the UGCC, which all contemptuously abstained.

The congress demanded the establishment of a regime of total domestic autonomy based on the parliamentarian model of Westminster and operating in the framework of the Commonwealth.[46] In a telegram to the Secretary of State in London, it denounced the incompatibility of the Coussey constitution with the needs and wishes of the clear majority of the population and thus asked for it to be abolished.

On December 15, by order of the CPP's central committee, Nkrumah informed the governor that a campaign of non-violent civil disobedience would soon be launched if authorities continued to ignore the amendments passed by the Constitutive Assembly of the People. From a legal standpoint, Nkrumah and his party seemed overconfident. But by their reckoning, it was a political struggle, and the ends often justified the means.

The same day, on the front page of the *Evening News* newspaper, he urged the people to prepare themselves for any eventuality and gave the administration a deadline of two weeks. To assure popular support, he made a tour through the regions. He observed with joy that the "people were ready for revolution." The atmosphere was becoming a powder keg that could explode at any moment.

Without delay the colonial authorities moved to the offensive. On the lookout, security forces patrolled the neighborhoods, kept surveillance on public demonstrations and summarily arrested CPP sympathizers. Police inspectors made daily searches of the party and union offices. The prosecutor filed suits against the newspapers of the CPP and Nkrumah was ordered to pay a fine. The secretary general of the government directly threatened him with insubordination and violation of state security. In a campaign of systematic misinformation, the radio broadcast announcements about the abolition of the campaign of civil disobedience and urged people to put their faith in the government. Governor Arden-Clarke had made up his mind to triumph.

With the failure of negotiations between the Meteorological Employees' Union and the administration, the social climate became more volatile. In spite of Nkrumah, the fire broke out. A strike was declared on January 6, 1950. Many people were arrested. As the governor refused to amend the constitution, the militants sprang into action. The CPP, along with the general union of workers, decreed a general strike on January 8. In Nkrumah's words, this was the beginning of the political and social revolution which would change the course of history for the Gold Coast and launch a great pan-African movement.

FROM THE DUNGEON TO TRIUMPH

The campaign of misinformation conducted by the government seems to have borne fruit in the cities at the beginning of this period of unrest. Nkrumah observed as early as January 10 a decrease of popular support in Accra. It would be erroneous, however, to think that this situation indicated an absence of leadership and ideology. Bob Fitch and Mary Oppenheimer were mistaken when they wrote that the campaign suffered this setback and so "got off to a bad start."[47]

To respond to the misinformation, Nkrumah traversed the city, dressed in a *fugu* or *batakari*, an ample, sleeveless shirt of thick cotton from the North worn by the Asante during military campaigns. In a lively and spirited voice, he harangued the crowds at the great crossroads before making up his mind to hold a lecture at the Arena. Many people came. After two hours of impassioned rallying, trust was reborn, the commitment was renewed and the battle would continue.

On January 11, the boycott of stores, rail and road blockades, the suspension of maritime activities at the docks and the strike of civil servants paralyzed economic and administrative life. Thus, that evening the governor instituted a state of emergency across the entire expanse of the territory and imposed a curfew in the large cities.

All meetings were forbidden, the publication of opposition newspapers was halted and complete censorship was imposed. A new force of mobile police, responsible for curbing mobs, roamed the neighborhoods. The leaders of the CPP were arrested at Kumase, Sekondi to the west of Accra, and other locales. They were charged with endangering the security of the state. Next, they came for the union leaders and the editors of CPP newspapers. The veteran's delegation was arrested on their way to a scheduled meeting with the traditional chiefs.

The government gave special authorization to all whites, including Syrians, to serve in security services. Wanton violence reigned. Arrests continued. Kojo Botsio, secretary general of the CPP, was in turn arrested. The governor wanted to create a void around Nkrumah to demoralize and weaken him before capturing him.

The height of violence was reached when two police officers were killed in a veteran's demonstration at Accra. The police net was tightened around militant groups. The other members of the CPP's central committee were taken. Finally, on January 22, Nkrumah was himself arrested and imprisoned in James Fort at Jamestown on the edge of the sea, not far from the administrative quarter.

Brought before justice, Nkrumah was found guilty on three charges and condemned to three years of prison without parole. The governor refused to establish a board of appeals that could give an order to free the accused. Therefore, the experience would be grievous at Jamestown Fort, a former slave fortress that had been converted into a prison. The cells were real dungeons, hot and humid during the day, cold at night, always noxious and infested with rats, cockroaches, fleas, and mosquitoes. Nkrumah and his companions were mercilessly punished because of their "audacity and impatience."

The world inside the prison would make Nkrumah very sensitive to questions of justice and would bring him to oppose the death penalty and other inhumane punishments. The conditions of life in the James Fort prison were scandalous and shameful; ten people to a cell, without beds, light, sufficient food, and only one bucket for everyone's needs. The prisoners were treated like the basest of criminals. For the intellectual Nkrumah, the lack of paper, pencil and book was especially troubling. To communicate with Gbedemah and other free comrades, he had to resort to using toilet paper. This contact with the exterior world, and resulting political action, helped him to maintain physical and moral balance.

While Nkrumah was in prison, the governor prepared the grounds for elections under the new constitution. Behind bars, the president of the CPP would try to prove his party's popularity in the country. Above all, he wanted to thwart the machinations of the leaders of the UGCC and chiefs who aimed to control the new assembly and to assure their stranglehold on the country. No one found this decision strange, given that Nkrumah had taken a stance against the proposal for the constitution. But, as a shrewd strategist, he reckoned that it was perhaps easier to subvert the situation by participating in the elections rather than by boycotting them. He thus asked the secretary general Kojo Botsio, who was freed, to present candidates in all electoral precincts. Nkrumah declared himself a candidate in Accra.

On "J" day, February 8, 1951, Kwame Nkrumah's destiny played out. The electors went to the ballot boxes and voted in great number. It was a memorable date in the history of nationalism in the Gold Coast. To the great surprise of everyone, the CPP's slate returned a resounding victory, with thirty-four seats out of thirty-eight. Winning 22,780 votes out of 23,122 in Accra, the prisoner Nkrumah dominated the candidates named there. He already had the reputation as the leader of a unique party whose members were unified and eschewed "tribalism." It was a stinging defeat to those who believed they had been born to lead the country, and who had already ordered ceremonial suits from London and had even sent their wives to take etiquette courses.

On February 12, 1951, at the entrance of James Fort, a human tide awaited the famous prisoner. For many hours, the chief of staff and the party members waited *en masse* to welcome him. He emerged, frail, bearded, and unshaven, his clothes in rags and holding in his hand notes written on toilet paper. What a spectacle! This man, in a wretched condition, symbolized the aspirations of this entire people. No one doubted his charisma; his image blended increasingly with that of the country.

When Nkrumah crossed the prison doorway, the crowd surged like a wave. At once, they lifted him up and carried him on their shoulders. This world saw him, watched him, and admired him as a brother and guide. All these people, men and women, adults and children, greeted his liberation with cries and applause that reverberated everywhere. They placed him in a convertible car, and with a retinue on foot trailing behind, snaked slowly through the streets like a powerful python, toward the Arena, the party's birthplace.

There, according to the country's tradition, they sacrificed a sheep to thank God and their ancestors and to wish health and welcome to the "guest of honor." Nkrumah placed his feet seven times in the warm flowing blood. Kwame would never forget this day. It was his triumph and his most beautiful experience of liberty, as he wrote: "This was the greatest day of my life, my day of victory and these were my warriors. No general could have felt more proud of his army and no soldiers could have shown greater affection for their commander in chief."[48]

The next day, Nkrumah accepted the governor's invitation without resentment for the treatment he had received in prison. The two leaders had a cordial discussion. The former prisoner was called to form the next government. He accepted the offer despite the inherent risks—the governor named the finance, security, and justice ministers—and he was recognized as the "chief of government affairs" instead of prime minister.

Kwame Nkrumah, U. K. Prime Minister, and others in Ghana,
ca. 1960.

Nevertheless, as a good tactician Nkrumah thought that "it was necessary to gain political power first." This was an important point of his doctrine. He sought to change the course of history and to help the people control their destiny. From his perspective, political power played a fundamental role in the transformation of society. Whoever held power could change economic structures and create a new order.

To show his faith in the country's unity, Nkrumah chose, in addition to his five partners in the CPP, two other ministers, one from the Asante region and a president of the assembly from the North, all of whom belonged to other organizations. He set the cabinet on the "path of liberation for Ghana and West Africa." He encouraged, in vain, the opposition party leaders and traditional chiefs to hold discussions and to get along on the basis of total and immediate autonomy. His government was making strides towards administrative reform to facilitate the Africanization of the executive branch and to strengthen regional democratic spirit. He also developed an investment plan to assure a greater exploitation of resources.

The Gold Coast Cabinet, Left to right front row: Hon. A. Casely-Hayford, Hon. Kojo Botsio; The Prime Minister, Hon. Kwame Nkrumah; Hon. K.A. Gbedemah, Hon. E. O. Asafu-Adjaye. Left to right back row: Hon. J.H. Allassani, Hon. N.A. Welbeck, Hon. A. Ofori Atta, Hon. Ako Adjei, Hon. J.E. Jantuah, Hon. Imoru Egals. Gold Coast, Accra.

Nkrumah was no less active in his foreign affairs. Convinced that West African unity was a necessity for which the grounds needed to be prepared, he visited Côte d'Ivoire, Guinea, and Liberia to strengthen relations with his neighbors. With emotions running high, he returned to Pennsylvania in the United States to receive an honorary doctorate at Lincoln University and followed by discussions with politicians and American industrialists about investment opportunities in Ghana. Even then, the plan for a hydroelectric dam on the Volta was already close to his heart.

From 1951 to 1953, the question of independence and unity preoccupied Nkrumah. Conservatives did not make his task easy. In the Asante region, the situation was growing worse. Cocoa producers were not happy with the purchase price of their product or with the policy of replacing aged shrubs or shrubs infested with noxious fungus that threatened the plantations. These planters thought that they were poorly represented at the Commercialization Fund for cocoa and that the government was punitively lowering the prices because of their support of the opposition. The price drop, linked to the international outlook, led to a malaise in the rural areas as well as in the cities. And yet, as a highlife song captures, cocoa was king in the central regions:

> If you want to educate children, it's cocoa
> If you want to build a house, it's cocoa
> If you want to marry, ah, you need cocoa
> If you want to buy clothes, cocoa
> If you want to buy a car, cocoa
> If you want to do something in this world,
> You need money, and so cocoa
> Cocoa, Cocoa, Cocoa[49]

These difficulties explain the formation of the National Liberation Movement (NLM) under the aegis of Kofi Busia and Danquah. From aristocratic backgrounds, these two received the "benediction of the council of Asante chiefs" and an immediate financial assistance of 20,000 sterling pounds (about 40,000 dollars or 10 million CFA at the time). The aristocracy used the cocoa crisis, which was the most vital commodity, to protect itself against what Baffour Osei Akoto, the great "Master of the Word" of the Asantehene, called "banditry, communism, gangsterism, and a lack of respect for the legitimate chiefs."

Although it carried the name of "movement," the NLM behaved like a genuine political party in the service of the moneyed bourgeoisie and landed aristocracy. For proof, it asked for the direct participation of the Asantehene, the Asante chief-king, in national affairs and especially in discussions about constitutional reform. In the name of this great dignitary the leaders of the NLM addressed a telegram to the queen of England to ask for the creation of a "royal commission" tasked with establishing a federal constitution that respected the rights of each region of the territory.

Nkrumah and his government had to deal with serious resistance. But they benefited from the support of the people of Kumase and of plantation workers. The latter rejected the NLM as "mate meho," that is, a separatist group.[50] Therefore, despite the origin of its leaders, the NLM did not achieve great popularity. Busia, the national president of the opposition, did not manage to block the march towards autonomy and unity, despite his alliance with leaders in the North.

The Northern region was isolated, culturally, and economically. For a while its representatives at the assembly had supported Nkrumah. But they ended up creating the Northern People's Party (NPP) to better control and develop their region. Unlike Busia's NLM, the NPP was more regional than "tribal." It included representatives from all the communities in the North regardless of ethnic or religious origin. Nkrumah and Busia both tried to attract its followers. They did the same with the organizations in the former British Togo.

At the same time, certain Muslim leaders were beginning to use their region for political ends despite the absence of social unity in their community. For a long time, the Muslim Association consisted of two main factions. The first included mostly Zarma expatriates, formerly established or recently arrived from the French colony of Niger. The second group was composed of the Hausa coming from Nigeria. Guided by the CPP, this group of young people opposed the rich and powerful traditional leaders, such as the Imams of Accra, Kumase, Takoradi and Tamale. They were transforming the Muslim Association into a Muslim Party that, in alliance with the NLM, was unleashed on Nkrumah.

In sum, there were several disparate currents that appeared in opposition to Nkrumah's unitary movement. The critical issues posed by these factions needed to be urgently addressed at the time of the 1954 elections won by the CPP. After the elections, Nkrumah dedicated himself, body and soul, to negotiating with the different factions to forge a national consensus.

In 1954 the CPP remained the dominant party in the Gold Coast, wielding 72 seats against 32 for all the opposition parties. This victory allowed for the creation of a new constitution, more democratic and more geared toward independence. From 1954 to 1956, clashes between political groups erupted in the North, in former British Togo, and in the central region. On all fronts the opposition wanted to prevent Nkrumah from holding talks with London about the means of independence.

The struggle for power became intense. As the first order of business, Nkrumah tried to negotiate with the opposition, but the leaders rejected the united front. Busia, Danquah and the chiefs were more than ever devoted to the formation of a federal state within which each region would be autonomous. Nkrumah led a bold campaign against this movement, and won the elections in 1956. Thus, the independence movement under the umbrella of unity prevailed. Strengthening the march towards unity, British Togo stayed with "Ghana" through the referendum organized by the U.N.

The British government thus accepted the negotiations with the aim of transferring power to Nkrumah's government. Independence was inevitable, and a new state would be born—Ghana—a name that all the leaders accepted despite their differences.

With independence in March 1957, as Dr. Kwame Ninsin has noted, the government would still be able to promote a policy of unity.[51] Taking advantage of his immense popularity, Nkrumah created structures to avoid fragmentation. In 1958, the constitution was thus revised. The chiefs, who up to then enjoyed important prerogatives, saw their power reduced. From that point on, they could not check any governmental decision or oppose the elected people of the nation. With this weakening of the bases of opposition, Nkrumah could devote himself to the task of the development of Ghana and carry on with his policy of African unity, his great dream.

4

THE MECHANISMS OF NKRUMAH'S AFRICAN POLICY

*As I drove home, physically and mentally tired but indescribably happy
and content, I reflected on the long and difficult road on which we had
travelled towards the goal of independence. African nationalism was not
confined to the Gold Coast—the new Ghana. From now on it must be
Pan-African nationalism, and the ideology of African political
consciousness and African political emancipation must spread throughout
the whole continent, into every nook and corner of it.*

*I have never regarded the struggle for the independence of the Gold Coast
as an isolated objective but always as a part of a general world historical
pattern. The African in every part of this vast continent has been
awakened and the struggle for freedom will go on. It is our duty to offer
what assistance we can to those now engaged in the battles which we
ourselves have fought and won. Our task is not done and our safety not
assured until the last vestiges of colonialism have been swept
from Africa.[52]*

—*Kwame Nkrumah*

THE CELEBRATIONS OF INDEPENDENCE

On Monday, September 17, 1956, Kwame Nkrumah was full of joy
when Governor Charles Arden-Clarke had him read the dispatch
that he had just received from London. In response to the request
of the Prime Minister of the Gold Coast, the British government
would grant independence as a united state on March 6, 1957. At
the spread of this news, there was a spontaneous celebration at the

Assembly, in the streets of Accra and in every corner of the country. The path had been long, but the next exhilarating stage would be longer still, as Nkrumah suggested in the preceding lines.

Kwame Nkrumah as Prime Minister of Ghana.

At the approach of the festivities, the city of Accra donned its most beautiful finery. The public works department repainted buildings, enlarged the main roads and decorated the parks. On the large avenue of independence, a grand luxury hotel for distinguished guests was inaugurated. Each day, preparations intensified. From mid-February, the city was literally taken by a storm of visitors from within the country and from abroad. The entourage of traditional kings and chiefs was marked by their golden *kente* cloth, their imposing English limousines or their long American cars with glistening chrome. The atmosphere was festive. The young progressives danced all night long to the cadenced and spellbinding rhythms of highlife or calypso, tunes characterized by the fusion of African style with a style imported from the Caribbean. It was the first celebration of independence in black Africa and the leaders of the Gold Coast wanted to set an example.

On February 26, preparations began to receive delegations from the 56 nations invited to attend the birth of the new state. Festivities of every kind—beauty pageants, bicycle races, horse riding, soccer matches, religious ceremonies in the churches and mosques; official dinners at the homes of the governor and prime minister; and the inauguration of new amphitheaters at the university, monuments for the dead, the Black Star Square, and the National Museum—all this drew the attention of visitors.

Among the great personalities who came were the Duchess of Kent, who would preside over the ceremonies in the name of the Queen of England; Richard Nixon, Vice President of the United States; Ralph Bunche, the Under Secretary of the United Nations (U.N.) and an African American diplomat who was representing the secretary general of the U.N.; Habib Bourguiba, President of Tunisia, which had just achieved independence; François Mitterand, Minister of Justice and Attorney General, leader of the French delegation; W.E.B. Du Bois, Martin Luther King, George Padmore, C. L. R. James and many other leaders of the pan-African movement. Nicholas Grunitzky, head of the government of Togo under French supervision, and his compatriot, opposition leader Sylvanus Olympio, as well as Felix Houphouët-Boigny, member of the French National Assembly from Côte d'Ivoire, were also invited. Houphouët's absence was notable. Also absent was Egyptian President Gamal Abdel Nasser who was not invited by the British government owing to a rupture in diplomatic relations after the Suez crisis in 1956. For Nkrumah, these celebrations confirmed the maturity of Africans.

Starting from the night of March 5, a dense crowd gathered along the sea across from the parliament in an old polo field in the elegant neighborhood located between James Fort and Christiansborg Castle. From the traditional dignitaries' section, representational music from the different regions of the country could be heard. In the middle of the green polo field stood two elegant platforms. On one, the military brass band in ceremonial garb played highlife tunes. It was a starry tropical night, magnificent and memorable.

At midnight on the hour, Kwame Nkrumah mounted the other platform, followed by members of his government, all dressed like prisoners in memory of their imprisonment. There was a moment of silence. Nkrumah rose, full of determination, dignity, and humility. The spotlights, installed on the roofs of the buildings, followed his slightest movements. He lifted his arms in a sign of victory, and with a loud and enthusiastic voice, he proclaimed: "Freedom for Ghana, Ghana is free forever!" And then, with feeling and joy he burst into tears. Then arose the sounds of the martial music, accompanied by the crowd's cries of joy and the beat of *donno* talking drums and drums of war from the entourage of the traditional chiefs. The celebration continued all night.

*Queen Elizabeth II of England and Prime Minister
Kwame Nkrumah.*

On the morning of the next day, March 6, the ex-governor Charles Arden Clarke took his oath as governor-general of Ghana and representative of Her Majesty the Queen of England before the Duchess of Kent and a mixed and multi-racial crowd. Next the Duchess proceeded with the ceremonial inauguration of the Ghanaian parliament. The symbols of sovereignty were exchanged: The Union Jack, flag of the United Kingdom, was lowered with grace and dignity and replaced by the national colors of Ghana—red, yellow, green—with a black star in the middle. The crowd sang the national anthem "Ghana Arise!" followed by the song of the CPP "There is Victory for us." A long procession closed the celebrations. A page had been turned. A new era was rising, full of hope and uncertainty.

NKRUMAH'S FOREIGN POLICY

The celebration of Ghana's independence took place during the so-called Cold War between the capitalist Western world and the Marxist soviet bloc. The possession of nuclear armament was at that time considered the driving force in international relations. As the eighty-first member of the U.N., Ghana joined a group of states that were relatively recently independent, African-Asian or third world countries, weak on the military and technological levels, but sovereign. The lack of balance between industrial countries and less developed ones was another feature of the international scene.

This imbalance did not escape Nkrumah. He wanted to work with the leaders of other African-Asian countries to bring a new model of power to the political scene. Collectively they believed that in contrast with the diplomacy being applied by the two great blocks, "force alone" was not sufficient for dominating the international arena. For them, a new force, based on morals, must be the decisive factor in international relations. Though it was an imponderable and intangible thing, moral force could be applied to all states, whatever their ideology. For in theory morality underlay all political actions. In this respect, it could create a new atmosphere, more conducive to peace in the world, while affirming the right of small countries and encouraging decolonization and respect toward non-European cultures.

With his African and Asian counterparts, Nkrumah wanted to reform international policy and to make the U.N. the organism *par excellence* in the service of peace free from the influence of the material power of member countries. Therefore, he attached so much importance to the U.N. Right or wrong, he dreamed that when many other colonies became independent, this organization could become the arena for dialogue and the center of a new international order. This vision required the creation of an appropriate policy on the African as well as the foreign fronts. To understand the implementation of the dream of unity, the central tenets of Ghana's foreign policy must be analyzed.

From the moment of independence, the Ghanaian government sought to define what it meant by "national interest" in foreign relations. The question was critical. It did not necessarily suggest a logical relationship between domestic and foreign policy. To clarify this point, many analysts have proven that Nkrumah's foreign policy affected Ghana's domestic policy much more than the reverse.

Unlike President Sékou Touré, for example, Nkrumah did not completely change his foreign relations based on the conduct of his national "adversaries." He was guided by a principle, a true common thread, which eventually, it must be said, ended up having repercussions on the way in which Ghanaians evaluated his leadership. For him, Ghanaian national interest, which demanded the well-being of the citizens and the achievement of major projects, such as the Volta dam giving electricity to several neighboring countries, was not contrary to African unity. According to his perspective, unity was a condition for achieving the national interest.

In Ghana, as elsewhere, foreign policy was based on achieving strategic or economic objectives or on ideological and cultural considerations. Apart from Togo, which Ghanaian leaders would have been willing to annex, Ghana was not engaged in imperialism. It did not seek to control the market or the resources of another country. On the contrary, from the very beginning, Nkrumah had a clear vision about Africa's future, as the quotation at the beginning of this chapter illustrates.

The cultural and political foundation of African self-awareness—pan-Africanism—remained the basic principle of Nkrumah's African policy from 1957 to his fall in 1966. During these nine years, he put everything into motion to achieve the goal he assigned himself: African unity. He believed unity was capable of radically changing political and economic conditions across Africa to the great benefit of all. His African policy was conceived in this light. In turn, this policy significantly oriented his attitudes towards the great powers. The Congo crisis and the difficulties of establishing pan-Africanism, or the obstacles against African unity itself, would draw Nkrumah, with each passing year, closer to the Marxist, Soviet and Chinese bloc.

Under Kwame Nkrumah, especially during the first five years of his regime, Ghana played a leading role on the international scene, but not because it was the first independent black state. For example, W. Scott Thompson thought that this role was considerable for a country of under seven million people.[53] Indeed, between 1957 and 1965 it was exceptional for a newly independent country to achieve so remarkable a visibility. Accra was then the capital, or even the Mecca, of the liberation movement and of militant pan-Africanism. At the U.N., Ghanaian diplomats were heard and their stances were respected. Along with Nasser, Sukarno of Indonesia, Nehru of India and Tito of Yugoslavia, Nkrumah figured among the great historical leaders of the Third World and of the Non-Aligned Movement. But what was the source of his international celebrity?

Indian Prime Minister Nehru, President Kwame Nkrumah, Gamal Nasser of Egypt (United Arab Republic), President Sukarno of Indonesia, and President Tito of Yugoslavia, in New York, ca. 1960.

Aside from Kwame Nkrumah's intrinsic qualities and those of his collaborators (to whom we will return), it is important to emphasize the economic conditions of Ghana on the eve of independence in 1957. According to all observers, this country was starting off on the right foot. It was the leading producer of cocoa, and one of the five major producers of gold. Moreover, with its cash reserves of over 500 million dollars, it ranked among the wealthy states.[54] These are exceptional conditions for a newly independent country of modest size. To be sure, Ghana had not gotten off to a bad start.

All of this implied that Nkrumah had the available means to conduct an independent foreign policy and an African policy in particular. In these prosperous years, he did not depend on any foreign aid. He was free to choose his political direction in his own time. Many African heads of state did not enjoy this advantage.

Ghana could then fashion a policy for its means because it had the means for its policy. Nkrumah could also count on a team of Ghanaians and competent foreign advisers and on a sound and capable administration. In these Cold War years, such a state, governed by an intelligent and educated man, could exercise influence. But the international political scene in general and the African scene in particular were at once complex and changing. With new independence for "nations," questions of borders would take on importance; a form of nationalism that was territorial rather than pan-African would develop; and the opposition between the leaders would increasingly take the form of a conflict between states. The African scene looked like a chessboard where many interests were at stake. It remained to be seen how the "pilot" would go about it and how he would fly over, if he could, the turbulence that hindered the route. Was the aircraft in good running order, so as to confront all the obstacles and finish the course in record time, as the captain wished?

In foreign policy, success depended not only on the qualities of the head of state and his staff, and the foreign affairs ministry, but also on the nature of the questions in play and the harmony that exists between the principal agents tasked with executing policy. In the following section, we attempt to apply these principles to the man himself.

Since we lack an exhaustive biography covering the years from independence to the *coup d'état* in 1966, it is not easy to speak of Nkrumah's personality as Head of State. Indeed, his autobiography was published in 1957, and no new edition treated his years in power. And yet power, if it does not transform the human being, at least tends to reveal undiscovered facets of the personality. Discussing this is also difficult because of the slightly enigmatic character of the person and because of the controversial myth surrounding him.

For many Africans, the name Kwame Nkrumah evokes a demiurge dedicated entirely to the cause of liberation, unity and the anti-imperialist struggle in order to give Africa a broad influence on the international stage.[55] Conversely, for others, he was an intolerant zealot, a dreamer and idealist who wanted to jump the gun, a leader incapable of satisfying the immediate needs of his people and a man who squandered his country's resources in order to sow subversion elsewhere in the name of a so-called socialist revolution.[56] The truth about Nkrumah lay somewhere between these two extremes. Whatever the case, a certain number of tangible facts help the analysis of how Nkrumah's attitudes affected his foreign policy.

On the eve of Ghanaian independence, Kwame Nkrumah uttered two key sentences that posterity remembered: "Our task is not finished and our security is not assured so long as the last vestiges of colonialism have not been swept away from Africa." The second is still more explicit: "The independence of Ghana has no value so long as the rest of Africa is not free." This is an oath that very few African leaders kept, but for Nkrumah it was a mantra. Unequivocally, his obsession was to create in his lifetime a united continental government in Africa and to contribute to the fight against colonialism and imperialism. Article II of the constitution declared still more explicitly the will of the people and government to "cede a part or the entirety of Ghana's sovereignty with the goal of union for African states."

To achieve this project, the statesman needed to synthesize all the different intellectual influences that had marked him, from idealism to Leninist practice. Nkrumah deserves to be considered the great nationalist of Ghana and Africa. His principal objective, which became his vocation, was the blossoming of his continent. It was a noble and generous thought. However, the facts revealed some problems. An enigmatic man, Nkrumah remained deeply attached to his ideas and thus appeared to discourage discussion. Moreover, when it came time to put his political project into effect, he seemed to favor the collaboration of foreigners over nationals.

Indeed, a good number of his immediate collaborators—including the most influential—were not Ghanaians. Did Nkrumah distrust his own countrymen? And why? In this case, what consequences would such behavior have on Ghanaians associated with the development of his foreign policy? Would Ghanaian ambassadors believe in their leader's pan-Africanism? This was an important question.

Another point to raise is the high degree of idealism and utopianism that Nkrumah possessed. For example, Thompson suggested that Accra's attitude in the Congo crisis is partially understandable considering the impact American internationalist President Woodrow Wilson exercised on the Ghanaian leader.[57] A former academic, liberal and optimist, Wilson fought after the First World War to create the League of Nations to stop any possible future wars. He held an unshakeable faith in international institutions and cooperation for the maintenance of peace.

In large measure, as Dr. Obed Asamoah has discussed, Nkrumah was a great partisan of the U.N. and of international institutions.[58] He appreciated the role that the U.N. played in decolonization and in regional unification. He thought that it could also contribute to unity by reinforcing cooperation between African member states. The confidence that he placed in the U.N. was so great that he seemed to forget that in the 1960s this organization remained an instrument in the service of the policy of western powers. It is difficult to think that the U.N., despite all of Nkrumah's speeches and those of other non-aligned leaders, could reinstall Patrice Lumumba or reestablish legitimacy in the Congo. It was not in the interest of the United States and its allies. Moreover, many African statesmen detected this same degree of idealism, if not lack of realism, in Nkrumah's pursuit of African unity. These are the questions that must be considered.

NKRUMAH'S COLLABORATORS

It is now important to say a few words about Nkrumah's administrative apparatus in the service of foreign policy. During the early years of independence, he simultaneously held the offices of prime minister and minister of foreign affairs. He was surrounded by two very important offices, the Secretariat for African Affairs and the Bureau of African Affairs. The Secretariat even worked at the president's residence, Flagstaff House, not far from Nkrumah's office. Attached to the presidency, it was responsible for coordinating all diplomatic affairs concerning Africa. For all practical purposes its prerogatives and prestige in this area were greater than those of the minister of foreign affairs.

As for the Bureau of African Affairs, it was an organization whose existence was mainly owed to the influence of George Padmore, Nkrumah's great counselor. It was a study center for contemporary African questions. After Padmore's death in 1959, the Bureau had the status of a non-governmental organization, independent of the minister of foreign affairs, but financed by Ghana. It reported directly to the president. Its function was to coordinate aid to liberation movements and all non-diplomatic organizations judged to be useful to the cause of liberation and unity. It was a pivotal instrument of foreign policy in general and African policy in particular.

Experience abroad had made it possible for Nkrumah to develop solid relationships with many people. Consequently, in 1957, he attracted counsellors of diverse origin and perspectives. For reasons that were at times personal and at others ideological, some of these individuals were entrusted with great responsibilities in the formulation and execution of foreign policy. For example, it is impossible to speak of African problems without mentioning the names of George Padmore, W. E. B. Du Bois, Samuel G. Ikoku, Timothy Bankole, Geoffrey Bing, General Henry Templer Alexander, Sir Arthur Lewis, Sir Robert Jackson, Erica Powell, and Conor Cruise O'Brien.

President Kwame Nkrumah at the home of W. E. B. Du Bois, on the evening of his 95th birthday, ca. 1963.

A few months after the independence festivities, to which he was formally invited, George Padmore returned to Accra as special counselor to Nkrumah on African affairs. He was believed to be second in command for Ghanaian foreign affairs. His influence, which roused jealousy in the circle of national diplomats, was deeply felt in the spheres of pan-Africanism and regional unions. The octogenarian Du Bois became a Ghanaian citizen and Director of Research for the *Encyclopedia Africana*, a vast historical project that would serve as a foundation in the struggle for unity. Samuel Ikoku, K. D. Gwira and Timothy Bankole were political refugees from Nigeria. A Marxist sought by the Nigerian police for treason, Samuel Ikoku worked as editor for *Spark*, the newspaper of the CPP. In 1961, Gwira became ambassador to Sierra Leone. Bankole coordinated the activities of the Secretariat and the Bureau of African Affairs. The ideology and actions of these refugees would have repercussions such as on Ghana's relations with the Nigerian Prime Minister, Alhadji Abubakar Tafawa Balewa.

As for the British expatriates in Nkrumah's circle, besides Geoffrey Bing and Cruise O'Brien, most were not known for social or radical ideas. Pan-Africanism did not particularly interest them, and it was a question whether they believed in it. Sir Anthony Lewis, general policy advisor, had already gone home in 1959 because his advice was no longer being followed. Sir Robert Jackson and his wife remained in Ghana until 1966, intimates of Nkrumah because of their experience in India and Pakistan and their expertise in international problems. Geoffrey Bing, former British parliamentarian, was Attorney General until 1961, before exercising a great influence in the Congo affair. For years, General Alexander served as chief of staff before leading the Ghanaian party in the Congo. Erica Powell, whom C. L. R. James found very devoted and loyal, found herself in one of the most sensitive positions as Nkrumah's private secretary. Conor Cruise O'Brien, an Irish diplomat with a good reputation as an international civil servant in the Congo, arrived in Ghana to assume the direction of the university. An admirer of Nkrumah's political thought, he played a noteworthy role until his departure in 1965.

Whatever their loyalty to Nkrumah, these foreign advisers posed problems. Some of them appreciated their "friend's" precision of vision; some lacked the courage to express their opinions, and others showed their hostility to any pan-African and anti-imperialist program. Most did not miss the opportunity to make severe judgments about him after his fall.[59] In many cases, their presence easily turned into a source of problems in the eyes of the native elite. Their immense influence made it difficult to create relationships between the Heads of State and the Ghanaian political elite. Probably Nkrumah's image suffered in consequence.

Among the numerous ministers and other dignitaries of the regime, Komla Gbedemah, Kojo Botsio, Nathaniel A. Welbeck, Ako Adjei and Kofi Baako were at the top of the list of Nkrumah's intimate collaborators. No one doubted their competence, although their behavior often raised questions. Moreover, in African politics one cannot omit the names of A. K. Barden, Tawiah Adamafio, John

Tettegah, Michael Dei-Anang, and Andrew K. Djin. Who were these great barons of the CPP?

Gbedemah, who studied economy in England, was an early collaborator. Minister of finances from 1954 to 1961, he encouraged foreign investments in Ghana rather than loans or gifts to "brother revolutionaries" of Africa. Kojo Botsio, an Oxford graduate who participated in the conference of Bandung, was much more interested in the pan-African cause than Gbedemah. From 1958 to 1959 and then from 1963 to 1965, as minister of foreign affairs, he played a role of the first order in formulating and executing African policy. Just like Gbedemah, Welbeck was a member of the central committee of the CPP since 1949 before becoming its secretary general. He was Ghana's first Ambassador to Guinea under the title "Resident Minister." Ako Adjei, former member of the UGCC which had invited Nkrumah in 1947, took charge of foreign affairs from 1959 to 1962, before being arrested in a plot to assassinate Nkrumah; he wielded a certain influence on the policy of union with Guinea, Mali, and Congo. Kofi Baako, one of his earliest collaborators, was for his part also a partisan of pan-Africanism and of a one-party system; he occupied different ministries and was temporarily the general secretariat of the CPP before assuming the office of minister of defense.

Aside from their nationalism and their experience in the struggle against the colonial regime, these great dignitaries had a hard time being part of a homogeneous team. A one-party system was not enough to create cohesion and unity among them. Each of them represented a faction within the CPP. Ministers like Gbedemah, Adjei and even Botsio seemed to share the opposition's opinions about questions of regional unity. They had little tolerance for the financial and material support that Nkrumah lavished on refugees and liberation movements. They were partisans of a pro-Western, moderate, and circumspect foreign policy in the African context. The lack of unity within the governing elite aggravated the problems that Nkrumah would encounter in his diplomacy. What's more, his diplomacy was no better served by the team of activists in the Bureau of African Affairs nor by the career diplomats.

After Padmore's death, Nkrumah entrusted the office's direction to A. K. Barden, former soldier who was noticed in the earliest years of the CPP. Barden regularly visited the "theaters of operation" in Africa and distributed necessary funds. His team included Tawiah Adamafio, former secretary general of the CPP and minister of state attached to the presidency; John Tettegah, former union president and itinerant ambassador; Andrew Djin, former businessman and ambassador to the Congo; and Michael Dei-Anang, writer and theorist of African policy. This group around Nkrumah ended up exercising an immense influence on foreign policy in general and on African problems in particular. Certain observers considered them "zealots" interested above all in maintaining their positions. Ghanaian career diplomats were unwilling to accept their autonomy and arrogance and held them responsible for the ultimate weakness of Ghana's foreign policy.

The leaders of Ghanaian nationalism had addressed the problem of training diplomats well before independence. In 1954, Nkrumah tasked Gbedemah, Botsio and Adjei with forming a committee for the selection of future diplomats. The candidates were chosen by a competition among the best heads of administration, all university graduates and competent in their respective domains. Among them were the economist F. S. Arkhurst, the former commander Seth Anthony, the economist and lawyer Alexander Quaison-Sackey, the specialist in administrative reform A. L. Busia, and university professor Kofi Busia. They were sent to London to follow specialized courses at the foreign office (Ministry of Foreign Affairs) before working in the field in British embassies in Latin America, Australia and elsewhere.

For these future Ghanaian diplomats, diplomacy was not extemporized, and the diplomats were not formed by an assembly line in party conferences or behind the scenes in military barracks. The idea of Foreign Service representatives without resources or a diplomat without a great education was foreign to their notion of the rules of diplomacy. For them, in every place and in every circumstance, the ambassador or attaché must represent their country with distinction.

These professional diplomats, some of whom would shine in the U.N. and in other international organizations, agreed with Nkrumah's foreign policy in the area of foreign investments. Nationalists and often wealthy men, they insisted on Ghana's standing and development. And so, they did not easily share the excessive policy of generosity toward African liberation movements. It should be highlighted that they were also products of British schooling and administration at its highest levels. Thus, it would be difficult for many of them to tolerate the increasingly anti-Western orientation of their leader and to understand the legitimacy of pan-Africanism as a doctrine of foreign policy. For the most part, unaware of the recommendations of the Manchester congress, they had one rather narrow idea about Ghanaian national interest. They had difficulty accepting that Ghana's future was inseparable from that of the rest of the continent. Their bitterness with respect to refugees and foreigners prevented them from dedicating themselves to a policy that they found controversial.

AN OVERVIEW OF THE OBSTACLES

Foreign policy is complex because it involves the interplay of several sovereign partners. For Africa, differences between states as well as problems of communication and language curb united movement. Thus, Nkrumah's African policy is understood better in light of regional geopolitics. The attitudes of the leaders of countries such as Togo, Côte d'Ivoire, Liberia, and Nigeria deserve to be taken into consideration, for they affected the way the leaders perceived Nkrumah and responded to his policy of unity. In general, they did not warmly approve of his enthusiasm for unity and revolution. A few examples suffice to explain this issue.

With Liberia or even Ethiopia, the differences stemmed from both ideology and diplomatic precedence. As President of the first African republic whose independence goes back to the nineteenth century, William Tubman hailed Ghana's arrival, but did not easily accept the preeminent place that Nkrumah immediately held on the international stage. In addition, their ideological concepts and vision of Africa's future were different. Tubman was not ready to acquiesce to Nkrumah's victory. In a certain measure, it was the same with Haile Selassie, emperor of Ethiopia and veteran of international politics since the 1930s. Togo presented a different problem.

Geographic proximity is very often an important factor in foreign politics, and the first diplomatic relations tend to secure borders. Thus, it is appropriate to look at Ghana's relations with Togo. Yet the common vote of 1956 organized by the U.N. resulted in the union of the formerly British Togo with Ghana. This was a defeat for Togolese nationalists especially for those under French supervision, who aimed for the reunification of the entire former German territory, or at least for the unity of the Ewe.

Indeed, Ewe irredentism, that is, the union of all peoples who are ethnically Ewe and living on the ridge between Togo and Ghana, was a problem from the first years of independence. As though to aggravate the situation, in April 1958, the Togolese union of Sylvanus Olympio, which was allied to the youth movement of Togo (JUVENTO), won the elections.

Relations between the two countries would then encounter difficult times due to Olympio's suspicion, probably legitimate, about Ghana's intentions, and because of Nkrumah's suspicions, no less founded, about France's presence in Togo. In any case, the Togolese leader's popularity at the U.N. and in Washington, and his policy of rapprochement with Dahomey (Benin) and other Francophone countries strengthened his position and obligated Nkrumah to adopt a *modus vivendi* with him. It remained to be seen whether Olympio and his successors would embrace an African governmental union under Nkrumah's leadership.

With Houphouët-Boigny, the problem was still more complicated. Despite their differences, Côte d'Ivoire and Ghana were genuinely sister countries in many respects, and Houphouët and Nkrumah cousins belonging to a large Akan family divided by colonial borders. Jon Woronoff insisted with good reason on this family tie.[60] But the two leaders had different temperaments and ideologies. Even if both had a militant and radical past, Houphouët-Boigny gave up his alliance with French communists early on to become the most influential African leader in Paris.

While Nkrumah was developing his plan for pan-Africanism and unity, Houphouët, who was one of the principal founders of the larger African inter-territorial movement known as the African Democratic Assembly (*Rassemblement Démocratique Africain*-RDA), did not easily tolerate the idea of a federation of French West Africa, preferring instead independence and development within the limited framework of the territories. The vision of one was continental, while the vision of the other was "national." Nkrumah overlooked Nkroful, the village of his birth, while Houphouët put his, Yamoussoukro, on the world map. These differences were not slight.

Although Nkrumah and Houphouët had already met one another in 1947 when Nkrumah was visiting Paris, the political opposition between the two did not break until the occasion of Ghana's independence. In juxtaposition to the joy that Nkrumah took in independence, Houphouët immediately kept his distance, preferring cooperation with the metropole.

Observers gladly contrasted the champion of Gold Coast nationalism with Houphouët, the principal defender of the seemingly more materially promising Franco-African cooperation. For a long time, Houphouët served as advocate against independence in poverty. The opposition between these two plans for Africa's future appeared clearly in an article that Houphouët-Boigny published in the newspaper *Foreign Affairs* in July 1957:

> The example of the young state of Ghana is very tempting.... But the exercise of this power in a fashion consonant with national and human dignity is difficult... We have won a place in the history of France and of the free world. We do not want to abandon this recent heritage by trying to go back to our origins.[61]

The opposition to independence became an official party when the leader of Côte d'Ivoire received the prime minister of the Gold Coast at Abidjan during the same year. In his welcome speech to Ghanaians, Houphouët let fly these words, henceforth famous: "Let each of us make our experience in absolute respect of our neighbor's experience; and in ten years, we shall establish the balance of the comparison."[62] It is therefore difficult to imagine that Nkrumah and Houphouët-Boigny could come to an agreement on the question of an African continental government.

Border issues emerged and complicated interstate relations, especially between Côte d'Ivoire and Ghana. Jacques Baulin has shown with perspicacity how the difference of opinion between Houphouët and Nkrumah partly stemmed from the arbitrary nature of the borders separating their two countries.[63] Houphouët used to think that the president of Ghana was increasing instability or at least tension in the Agni region on the border separating their states. Nkrumah was accused of using the Ivorian Sanwi refugees living in Ghana to form a new political group that included all the different Akan peoples of Ghana. Let us recall that this was one of the chief accusations against Jean-Baptiste Mockey, the Ivorian leader of Sanwi or Nzema origin like Nkrumah. Moreover, the very strong French presence in Côte d'Ivoire did not reassure Ghanaians. Even if Houphouët believed in African unity, he did not extol Nkrumah's conception of it.

Because of its demographic and economic power, Nigeria is another case that must be considered when analyzing Nkrumah's African policy. Unlike the nationalist veteran Nnamdi Azikiwe, the two other main Nigerian leaders, Obafemi Awolowo and Alhadji Abubakar Tafawa Balewa, were very early critics of Nkrumah's "pretensions." Even before their independence, they had difficulty understanding why the Republic of Ghana was communicating via the Foreign Office to deal with them. This diplomatic rule seemed to them a "superiority complex" on the part of Ghanaians. Then, after Nigeria's independence, they did not easily tolerate Nkrumah's radicalism and support of Nigerian extremists.

For the authorities of Lagos, the problem was summed up in one sentence: "Either Ghana works with us, or we are opposed to it on the African stage." This was then very serious. How could Nkrumah "appease" Nigerians and involve them in the project of African unity as he conceived it? That was the question.

Africa was not isolated. It formed an integral part of the world. It affected international politics as much as international politics affected it. Consequently, Nkrumah's success depended in part on the international context. His African policy took shape when the great powers were for their own reasons interested more and more in Africa. African leaders, exposed to competition between the two blocs and even to divergences within each of the two ranks, tried to conduct a somewhat clever policy of non-alignment.

The arrival of President Kwame Nkrumah to the Non-alignment movement conference, Belgrade, ca. 1961.

And yet Kwame Nkrumah was known for his pan-African, anti-colonial and anti-imperialist ideas. Gradually, he supported socialism. He did not easily accept many aspects of French policy, including nuclear tests in the Sahara, the boycott of Guinea, the Algerian war and even the idea of a Franco-African community. Although he admired cooperation based on multi-racialism and the sovereignty of member states, which was characteristic of the Commonwealth, he denounced English policy in Rhodesia (Zimbabwe) and in South Africa. A disciple of American federalism, he did not hide his discontent with the United States' actions in the Congo. Interested in the revolutionary character of Marxism, he had a hard time appreciating the timidity of the Soviets on the international scene. In sum, Nkrumah could easily make powerful enemies for himself.

The interference of the great powers in African affairs and the dependence of numerous states on their former mother countries made Nkrumah's task still more difficult. Yet, the politics of African unity transcended the continental context. His enthusiasm for forging a continental government, which many observers considered a rashly conceived illusion, clashed with the sensibilities of these heads of state with whom he could build unity. Did his partners share his engagement? Did the speed he imposed seem to them too fast? Whatever the case, Nkrumah's African policy consisted, on the one hand, of remaining faithful to his doctrine and on the other, of trying to work together with his adversaries. In sum, it was a policy of compromise that was hard to achieve. The great African conferences, the attempts at union and the Congo crisis helped to better clarify the situation.

5

ATTEMPTS AT REGIONAL UNION AND
THE DREAM

Not far from the president's residence in Accra, at the crossroad of the Avenue of Independence and the circular boulevard Ring Road Central, now called Thomas Sankara Square, once stood a large statue which General Afrifa's soldiers demolished. It was an abstract and splendid work, with three elongated wings, pointing in different directions, symbolizing the Union of Ghana, Guinea, and Mali, one of the first examples of regional reorganization in Africa.

From 1957 to 1966, Nkrumah conducted intense diplomatic activity and made himself as many admirers as he made enemies. Significant funding and logistical support went from Ghana to the nationalists of southern Africa. Students and refugees of these countries received scholarships to Ghana and abroad, while their soldiers were instructed in guerilla warfare. Nkrumah was known as the great champion of liberation and independence; and African students widely read his writings. In the president's mind, these considerations and activities could contribute to the creation of African unity and the establishment of socialism for development. This chapter examines the pan-African conferences and attempts at reorganization to illustrate both the blossoming of Nkrumah's dream and the weaknesses in the execution of his project.

FIRST CONFERENCE OF INDEPENDENT AFRICAN STATES

During the independence celebrations, Nkrumah held talks with representatives of African states concerning international problems and the need to forge an African perspective in foreign politics. In this way, the idea of a conference of independent states materialized. According to the Ghanaian diplomat Alex Quaison-Sackey, it was Nkrumah himself who took the initiative for the plan.[64] To avoid sensitive issues and to assure the success of his plan of unity, he wanted to work with his peers and to collect their consent. Diplomacy was necessary.

At the conference of the Commonwealth in April 1957, Nkrumah resumed discussions with authorized African ambassadors in Great Britain (South Africa refused to participate).[65] He urged them to develop the conference themes. In August 1957, the first meetings took place at the embassy of Sudan, despite Egypt's absence and the strident objections of the Liberians who wondered why Ghana alone was taking the initiative for this meeting (it was the beginning of Liberia's protracted distrust of Nkrumah). The meetings continued throughout the summer.

Later, the proposal of Ghanaians about the purpose of the conference emphasized the following ideas: the necessity of coordinating the politics of African states and of establishing immediately an effective mechanism of cooperation; and the need to consider the international arena in its relation to African interests and to accelerate the process of independence. The Liberian representatives were unsatisfied. They again tried to put a wrench in Nkrumah's plans by suggesting as a further order of business "non-interference in the affairs of other states and the repudiation of foreign ideas," which were thought dangerous. The proposition was rejected since each state had the right to choose its own ideology. They entered thus the second stage of preparing for the conference.

To demonstrate the interest he attached to the project, Nkrumah left nothing to chance. No one was neglected. All the heads of state were kept abreast of the plan. To assure the effective participation of Egypt, Nkrumah sent Ako Adjei to Cairo to hold talks with President Nasser. Soon after, Padmore and Adjei went to other capitals. They already observed that the other leaders did not keenly share the idea of a continental government. Padmore hoped that Nkrumah could show his peers the urgency of the issue. The Ghanaian diplomat, A. L. Adu, was named director of the secretariat responsible for organizing the conference.

On April 15, 1958, Kwame Nkrumah welcomed the delegations of seven African countries, in addition to that of Ghana, which had come to attend the First Conference of the Independent African States. With five delegations, North Africa dominated. It was the first time that representatives of sovereign states from both sides of the Sahara met to discuss African problems, reinforce their ties, reduce tensions and to struggle against "colonialism and racism."[66] Nkrumah's speech made no reference to the question of a continental government. Why? William Tubman of Liberia was the only head of state to attend the meeting, because Nkrumah's doctrine worried him. The Ghanaians were disappointed by the absence of Nasser and Haile Selassie. Thus, the discussions took place on the ministerial level and did not touch on the issue of unity, which was the remit of heads of state.

The final report, which was adopted on April 22, was in line with Nkrumah's views. The delegates were unanimous in supporting the struggle of liberation in Algeria. They also called for greater collaboration between independent states in the fight against racism, colonialism, and foreign interference. Egypt and Liberia opposed the establishment of the permanent secretariat that Ghana had proposed. They all accepted a compromise, creating a permanent secretariat of the conference among the ambassadors to the United Nations (U.N.). It was tasked with holding meetings in New York and organizing the next conference planned for Addis Ababa in 1960.

For most observers, this conference was a success for Nkrumah because of the impetus given to African liberation. His image in the public eye was crystalizing as that of a leader devoted body and soul to Africa's highest interests. The conference passed into history as a stage in the strengthening of African unity. To continue his momentum, Nkrumah took up his pilgrim's staff. Accompanied by Padmore and other advisers, he visited the seven countries that participated in the conference. This trip of nearly two months allowed him to get to know his peers and to meet the leaders of mass movements. He received a warm welcome everywhere, which nonetheless did not conceal the reservations of the leaders. The essential task was not solely to establish a dialogue with the leaders but also to take the pulse of the depths of Africa. And so, he planned another conference, even more magnificent, without the heads of state.

THE FIRST ALL-AFRICAN PEOPLES' CONFERENCE

From this point on, Nkrumah and his advisers wanted to orient their actions toward pan-Africanism, and thus the masses, in accordance with the spirit of Manchester. Thus, at the time of the constitutive congress of the African Regroupment Party (*Parti du Regroupement Africain*-PRA) in Cotonou in July, he supported the formation of an assembly made up of African peoples. But unlike the Manchester congress, the initiative for the new conference would come from Africans themselves and would prove their maturity. This conference would be called therefore the First All-African Peoples' Conference. Known today as the First Conference of African Peoples, it was the work of Padmore, to whom Nkrumah had entrusted the organization. The preparatory committee received the necessary funds from the Ghanaian government. In its effort to define Africa's evolution, the program proclaimed pan-Africanism as "an ideology of African, socialist, and non-violent revolution," despite Liberia's objections.

Around 300 representatives belonging to some 60 political and union organizations working in 25 countries gathered in Accra from December 6-13, 1958. Most of the Francophone leaders were absent. In contrast, Patrice Lumumba of the Belgian Congo (Democratic Republic of the Congo-DRC), Frantz Fanon of Algeria, Felix Moumié of Cameroon, Roberto Holden of Angola, Abdoulaye Diallo of Sudan (but in the service of Guinea), Tom Mboya of Kenya, Kenneth Kaunda of North Rhodesia (Zambia) and Bakary Djibo of Niger were present.[67] Mboya was elected president. Several observers and journalists came from the United States, Europe, and the Soviet Union. The agenda focused on non-violent political action, neo-colonialism, tribalism, racism, and the necessity of a common front for liberation and unity.

Prime Minister Kwame Nkrumah and Patrice Lumumba, future prime minister of Congo, ca. 1958.

On December 6, 1958, Nkrumah inaugurated the conference before a jubilant assembly. In his impassioned speech, he tackled colonialism, asked for independence for the territories still under colonial rule and denounced imperialism. The debates were heated. For instance, on the question of non-violence, Frantz Fanon and the delegates of the Maghreb who were fighting underground, attacked the arguments of the moderates. Nkrumah then displayed evidence of his great talent as a mediator. He received the delegates, held conversations with them and maintained a spirit of concord. He won the admiration of everyone for this. In short, it was due to Nkrumah that the conference was a success.

At the close of the congress on December 13, the delegates adopted resolutions that were generally favorable to Ghana's arguments.

For example, the first resolution, anti-colonial in nature, support-ed the cause of national liberation and put independent Africa on guard against associating with foreign powers under the cover of mil-itary and economic alliances. The delegates also accepted the use of force to obtain independence. The second resolution recommend-ed breaking off relations with South Africa and the withdrawal of South African supervision over the African southwest (Namibia). It also urged the creation of an "African Legion of Volunteers" for lib-eration.

The third resolution recommended the establishment of five large federations each covering the North, West, South, East and center of the continent. Unlike the idea of continental government, this resolution urged a regional approach. It was a compromise, because besides Ghana, no country still believed in the creation of a unitary government.[68] The conference established a permanent secretariat whose seat was fixed in Accra under the direction of the unionist and diplomat Abdoulaye Diallo. This body was responsible for coor-dinating anti-colonial political activities. According to all observers, this first pan-African conference was a success for Nkrumah. He had gained some believers and his ideas aroused interest everywhere.

Indeed, in many countries, lively political action followed the conference. For instance, upon returning to Leopoldville (Kinshasa), the delegates Patrice Lumumba and Cyrille Adoula, as well as Joseph Kasavubu who followed the works from afar, organized the first great demonstrations that would change the face of the Belgian Congo. The case was similar for participants who had come from central Africa. They drew from the conference a new strength to confront the discriminatory colonial regime of the Prime Minister Roy We-lensky, who would publicly accuse Nkrumah of sowing unrest in the Federation of Rhodesia.[69] This then was a great pan-African confer-ence. Now the attempt at regional political union that followed will be examined.

THE UNION BETWEEN GHANA AND GUINEA

Guinea's independence on October 2, 1958 represents a great date in the history of African nationalism. The young state's courage in the face of French hostility further increased its prestige. For these reasons, Nkrumah considered Guinea a natural ally. He renewed his contacts with Sékou Touré and invited him to Accra. The relations between the two leaders can be explained by recalling their political background.

Nkrumah and Touré both advocated independence in colonized territories and dreamed of African unity, each in their own way, as emerges from their writings and actions. It is unnecessary to return to the example of Nkrumah, which is analyzed in chapters 3 and 4. As for Touré, the referendum of 1958 shows his attachment to the ideal of independence and unity.[70] As he expressed it, "The Democratic Party of Guinea is searching for unity across the entire African continent, and particularly the Africa affected by French culture, namely the groups AOF and AEF, in order to approach tomorrow's United States of Africa, which will be the brilliant manifestation of our character in the community of free nations."[71]

Just like article two of Ghana's constitution, Article 34 of Guinea's first constitution stipulated that the Guinean state could renounce national sovereignty in favor of unity. In theory, Guinea's independence was placed in the service of unity. Indeed, as Touré further declared, "our freedom would lose its greatest significance if we had to limit it to the narrow confines of our own country."[72]

Unlike Nkrumah, however, Touré thought that African unity must be achieved gradually, for example, first between countries from similar colonial traditions. Under these conditions, French Guinea could not easily link itself with Anglophone Ghana. For Nkrumah, these differences seemed secondary. He wanted to advance quickly without consideration of colonial heritage. These points should be emphasized even though the two leaders felt it prudent to keep silent about them in October 1958.

The economic consequences of the Franco-Guinean crisis did not leave Sékou Touré very much space to maneuver. France increasingly cornered Guinea. Without offering himself to the highest bidder, Sékou Touré skipped over the possibility of cooperating with Nkrumah. Guinea quickly had to break its isolation as well as the embargo imposed by France. This imperative certainly drew Touré closer to Nkrumah. Thus, both felt the need for unity. Their opposition to balkanization further strengthened their ties, albeit only temporarily. Touré was already envisioning the rapprochement with Ghana when he declared in one of his first press conferences:

> Ghana is an African territory that certainly has the advantage of experience over us, since it attained independence well before us. It is quite natural for us to be able to draw from Ghana's experience, which is perhaps closer to Guinea's opportunities than the experience of other countries in other contexts. It is natural then for us to be able to have ties with Ghana.[73]

The initiative to form a union, however, came from Nkrumah. According to witnesses, he was overjoyed at Guinea's declaration of independence. In accordance with his principles, in order to realize his drams, he was committed to help and ally with this brother country.. This was his chance. He dispatched a goodwill mission to Conakry and presented Guinea's candidature to the U.N., a protocol that France refused to do. Later in October a delegation including Saifoulaye Diallo, president of the national assembly, Ismael Touré, minister of the interior, and Moussa Diakité, governor of the Central Bank, went to Accra and discussed cooperation with Ghana. Nkrumah promised as much aid as he could, a promise that was well worth the Guinean leader's journey.[74]

Thus, on November 20, 1958, accompanied by a large delegation, Sékou Touré arrived in Accra prepared to discuss anything that would help cement the union between the two states. Was it an act of opportunism or of conviction? The next day the secretary general of foreign affairs of Ghana, A. L. Adu, and the Guinean diplomat Telli Diallo, held discussions through an interpreter and adopted the text of a plan of cooperation. The minister of foreign affairs, Ako Adjei, reported that Touré wanted a direct political and economic alliance. Nkrumah warmly received the idea, but many among his advisers doubted the Guinean leader's sincerity. Despite everything, the union between Ghana and Guinea saw the light of day.

Nkrumah and Touré publicly announced the union between their two states on November 23, 1958. Several moments later, Ghana granted Guinea a loan of 10 million sterling pounds. But what was the real nature of the union? What did it really consist of? This was the question that people kept asking themselves.

The announcement from Accra was silent about the mechanisms of the association. For Nkrumah, it represented the nucleus of a still greater union to be formed among West African states. Despite their desire to harmonize their policies in the areas of defense and economic and foreign affairs, the two heads of state stressed that the agreement must not "carry prejudice against their present or future relations with the Commonwealth or the Franco-African community, respectively."[75] The union was not then complete. Mixed inter-ministerial committees were called upon to prepare in detail for the concrete aspects of the agreement. The ambassadors of the two countries took the title of resident ministers and were authorized to attend cabinet meetings.

Legally, the union had neither foundation nor structure. Nkrumah and Touré had hastily concluded a vague alliance. The union stemmed from the accelerated historical evolution that made Ghana and Guinea the first independent states in western Africa. For this reason, the two countries were a step ahead of the rest. Could they exploit the advance they had made? Were Nkrumah and Touré ready to "lay everything on the table"? Could the union, inscribed on paper, really achieve an effective integration?

Reactions to the union from both sides help reveal the problem that goodwill was unable to resolve. Before the National Assembly in Accra, Nkrumah expressed his joy at being an "instrument of unity" and at the same time his pride for "laying the foundation" of the continent's future greatness.[76] He also set about to furnishing the material aid that Guinea needed, despite opposition leader Kofi Busia's reluctance and the doubts of the finance minister Gbedemah.

Ghana was divided on the question. As the years passed, a deepening division would set professional diplomats and members of the

Bureau of African Affairs in opposition. For Nkrumah's supporters, the union represented an important political accomplishment, but for many Ghanaians, the loan of ten million sterling pounds seemed rash, premature, and dangerous even. Financial aid does not make unity, they thought. But Nkrumah did not budge. A man of principle, he was happy to see his dream take concrete form. In a personal message, Telli Diallo thanked him for his actions.[77]

As for Guinea, the reaction was complicated. In December 1958, a Ghanaian delegation led by the minister of finance and including the governor of the bank and other high-level offices held discussions at Conakry about the means of effecting the union and the loan. According to Ghanaian sources, "the Guineans are acting as if they were granting a favor to Ghana by allowing it to contribute to their treasury."[78] According to the same sources, Sékou Touré made the delegation wait for two and a half days before receiving them.

At the ministerial discussions that followed, an accord was reached about the means of disbursing the loan. One million would be paid out immediately as a first installment; then three million would be paid out during the first trimester of 1959, three million in 1960, and the rest in 1961. The loan was granted at the modest rate of two percent.

In the face of such commitment on the part of Ghana, the behavior of the Guineans seemed strange, to say the least. How can it be explained? According to the Guinean ambassador Achkar Marof, as one Ghanaian quoted him, the leaders of Conakry acted coldly due to the presence of white advisers in the delegation from Accra. But is this explanation satisfying? Let us note that at the same time a mission of French experts were holding discussions in Conakry about Guinea's association with the Franc Zone. These discussions resulted in the Franco-Guinean agreements on December 5, 1958, which were ratified January 7, 1959.[79] Sékou Touré seemed ready to involve himself in technical cooperation with Ghana, but not in union. At Conakry, the idea of a political alliance seemed like a novelty that had not yet taken shape. Touré considered Guinea a zone of French culture that would have difficulty "indenturing itself to a member country of the British Commonwealth." Already, the monetary question was an obstacle to union.

In addition, it is easy to underestimate the personalities of the two leaders. As is well known, Nkrumah and Touré both had strong personalities, commanding respect and naturally aspiring to embody power. In their own way, each represented the living symbol of nationalism for their countries and the aspirations of their peoples. They were both known for militancy and anti-colonialism. But was this enough to unite them within the same political body? The task was not easy. In the union, a conflict of leadership seemed hidden beneath the surface. It is difficult to imagine Sékou Touré effacing himself before Kwame Nkrumah due to his age or because of Ghana's economic superiority.

Nkrumah believed in the union, despite Guinea's desire to remain in the Franc Zone. To revive the plan, he sent his long-standing friend Nathaniel Welbeck to be resident minister in Conakry. Accompanied by a large delegation, Welbeck spent a week in Guinea. Optimism was reborn, and they believed that the union would be realized. Welbeck's sudden replacement by the former minister of foreign affairs, Ako Adjei, did not change the situation at all. The participation of Abdoulaye Diallo (resident minister of Guinea in Accra) in rallies and other demonstrations by the CPP strengthened their optimism.

When it came to diplomatic representation, however, a problem arose. As resident ministers, the ambassadors participated in cabinet meetings without restriction. In Accra, Diallo attended ministerial council meetings where, in conformity with the parliamentary nature of the regime, major decisions were made. He had access to documents but could not take them away. In sum, he was abreast of the government's decisions and the country's policy in general. For the Ghanaian ambassador at Conakry, things seemed different. In 1959, Guinea was already heading toward the state-party system in which the political office of the party was the central decision-making body. Not being a member of this body, the resident minister of Ghana was a bit marginalized.

To make their machine run without proper operating parts, Nkrumah and Touré had to travel and coordinate regularly. Nkrumah went to Conakry on April 23, 1959. For three weeks, he traveled the country and conversed with local leaders and religious chiefs, his acquaintances of old. His discussions with Sékou Touré gave birth to a document called the "Declaration of Conakry." In this brief document, they reaffirmed their support for the cause of African unity and promised to consolidate, in practice, the union between Ghana and Guinea. But what did they mean by "practice"? No one knew. It was known that diplomatic speeches often cloak the speakers' genuine intentions, and Nkrumah and Touré were not exceptions to the rule. The Declaration of Conakry recognized that each state held the right to maintain its own army and diplomacy. Each could then go it alone. Thus, the union came down to a very vague association without foundations or structure. In short, it had gotten off to a bad start. However, Nkrumah held firm to his dream of unity.

In 1959 West Africa counted only three independent states, Liberia, Ghana, and Guinea. The latter two had unceasingly discussed their project of union since November 1958. For Nkrumah, it would be ideal to include Liberia. The task was difficult because of President Tubman's distrustfulness. Tubman himself developed a vague plan for the association of African states. Then in July 1959, he invited his two counterparts to a discussion in Sanniquellie near Mount Nimba. In his opening speech, Tubman clearly disclosed his point of view. For him, any discussion about African unity could only be exploratory as it was necessary to wait for the independence of the colonized territories. In other words, Liberia opposed Nkrumah's plan.

Aside from this declaration, there was no mention of unity. Sékou Touré seemed even to incline toward a process of gradual regroupment without structure. In this respect, he followed Tubman, for whom the most practical method of reaching unity was to strengthen interstate cooperation, but without the transfer of rights of sovereignty. In sum, the conference of Sanniquellie intensified the gulf between Ghana and Guinea. It was a victory for Tubman (who would use the spirit of Sanniquellie to create the OAU). Despite every-thing, Nkrumah judged himself victorious insofar as he compelled the Liberians to become aware of unity. And so, he declared that Sanniquellie was like an "atomic bomb" that opened still wider per-spectives.[80] In truth, Nkrumah was too optimistic. The conference of ministers of foreign affairs of independent states at Monrovia, Au-gust 4-8, 1959, did not even address the question of African unity.

The Ghana-Guinea Union continued for better or worse. The leaders and their representatives visited one another periodically, and a semblance of technical cooperation was maintained. However, the emergence of Conakry as a second capital for liberation movements incurred umbrage at Accra.[81] The monetary problem would sound the union's death knell.

Guinea's withdrawal from the Franc Zone in 1960 could have led to a monetary union with Ghana, as was thought at Conakry. In May 1960, discussions opened on the question. Sékou Touré in-sisted on the immediate creation of the monetary zone. Minister Gbedemah and other members of the Ghanaian delegation were not ready to withdraw from the Sterling bloc or to shut the door on the Commonwealth. It was the divorce between the two countries. But in these years of independence, new perspectives were rapidly emerg-ing in Africa.

THE UNION OF GHANA, GUINEA AND MALI

The year 1960 was marked by great upheavals on the political scene in western Africa, as some ten countries gained independence: Cameroon, Côte d'Ivoire, Dahomey (Benin), Upper Volta (Burkina Faso), Mali, Mauritania, Niger, Nigeria, Senegal, and Sierra Leone. In this vast ensemble, balkanized after the collapse of the French and British colonial empires, the question of association and unity arose with urgency. All the leaders spoke of it. Would Nkrumah be able to exploit this situation? The states tended to associate with one an-other based on ideological and geographical affinities, as shown by the examples of the Federation of Mali and the Council of Accord (Conseil d'Attente).

In May of 1959, the Council assembled. It included Côte d'Ivoire, Dahomey, the Upper Volta and Niger. In many respects, it was very different from the union between Ghana and Guinea. Having minimal but functional institutions, the Council was seated with the heads of state, the ministers of common affairs and the presidents of national assemblies. The member states established a fund of solidarity to assist one another. A customs union was organized, and an amortization fund was created in the same monetary zone as the CFA. In sum, the political, economic, and military coordination between the four member states became increasingly powerful. The association was operational. Moreover, through the influence of President Houphouët-Boigny, the Council of Accord exercised influence on the general orientation of policy in the sub-region.[82] His relations with the leaders of Liberia and Nigeria left a lasting mark on African politics.

As for the Federation of Mali, it emerged in January 1959 following the disintegration of the federation of French West Africa. At the start, it included four countries: Senegal, Sudan (Mali), Dahomey and the Upper Volta. A few months later, under pressure from Houphouët-Boigny, Dahomey and the Upper Volta withdrew to join ranks instead with the Council of Accord. From that point on, the federation included only Senegal and Sudan, whose interdependence was symbolized by the Dakar-Niger railroad. With infrastructure inherited from the former federation of the AOF, of which Dakar was the capital, it possessed many institutions and specialized agencies that perhaps lacked flexibility at the time of political disintegration.

According to witnesses, the failure of the Federation of Mali had its roots above all in the differences between the two principal leaders, Modibo Keïta of Sudan and Leopold Senghor of Senegal. At the conference of Dakar in April 1960, their differences were exposed. The Federation broke up in August 1960 after what appeared to be an attempted *coup d'état*. From then on, each of the two partners followed its own path independently. Sudan kept the name of Mali and reexamined its options.

Unlike Sékou Touré, Modibo Keïta advocated an "yes" vote to the referendum of September 28, 1958. In working with other leaders in the context of the Franco-African Community, he hoped that a solution could be found to shore up the famous federation of the AOF. For him, federalism was a step in the path of African unity. And so, he gambled on the Federation of Mali. Mali's collapse was a huge defeat for him.

However, the collapse did not discourage Keïta entirely. France's complicity in this affair increased his anti-colonialist attitude and his determination for a solution of unity. "Mali continues," he declared at Bamako in September 1960 at the Extraordinary Congress of his party, the Sudanese Union (US-RDA). He further urged Africa to "resist the destructive action of the former colonial powers that desire to establish their domination."[83] Two ideas—opposition to France's nuclear tests in the Sahara and to its neo-colonialism as well as the vision of a new democratic and socialist society—became increasingly notable in Mali's ideology. These ideas would determine Modibo Keïta's attitude in the matter of regroupment.

Therefore, Malians did not join the Council of Accord, despite the advantages offered by Côte d'Ivoire after the closing of the Dakar-Niger railroad and despite personal relations between Houphouët and Keïta. Of all the West African parties, only the CPP and PDG shared the views and methods of the US-RDA. Political union thus seemed to be better oriented in this direction. The economic crisis following the collapse of the Federation of Mali accelerated the process by encouraging contact between Nkrumah and Keïta.

Already in July of 1960, a Ghanaian delegation directed by the resident minister at Conakry held a discussion with Modibo Keïta at Dakar. Keïta was invited to Accra at the beginning of September. The two leaders accepted the idea of a union of African states and promised to strengthen cooperation between their two countries. Nkrumah promised financial aid to Mali. Several days later, it should be noted, Gabriel d'Arboussier, acting as the head of a delegation from Senegal, was himself also at Accra to discuss the idea of an African community. But this initiative was unsuccessful because Nkrumah saw an ally in Keïta. In October, Mali and Ghana discussed diplomatic and commercial agreements at Bamako. In addition, Oumar Sow was quickly reassigned to his position as ambassador to Accra to help prepare for Nkrumah's official visit.

The Union of African States, also known as the Ghana-Guinea-Mali Union, represented by Kwame Nkrumah (middle), Modibo Keïta of Mali (left), and Sékou Touré (right) of Guinea.

At Bamako and in the provinces, Nkrumah received a very warm reception. Mali's impressive historical wealth reinvigorated his dream of unity. At Timbuktu and Gao, he fervently emphasized the historical bonds between the Nigerian savanna and the forest, and he invited the people of today to restore this community of shared tradition and destiny. Malians were not less eloquent in turn in their appreciation of the role that Nkrumah had played at the forefront of the African political scene since 1957. As the newspaper *L'Essor* wrote, "these gestures are such as Mali is not in the habit of forgetting."[84] Nkrumah unilaterally proposed that Ghana and Mali should have the same parliament. But it sufficed that the official announcement stated identical perspectives on all issues, including unity.

Meanwhile, Nkrumah, who was always looking to accomplish his dream, received the emperor Haile Selassie in December of 1960. Selassie presented his own plan for establishing the association of independent states of Africa after the fashion of the Arab League or the Organization of American States. Clearly, Nkrumah had difficulty selling his ideas to his peers and especially to his neighbors, whose influence risked thwarting his project. Of special concern were Houphouët-Boigny and Tafawa Balewa, two very influential men.

Nkrumah was very interested in Côte d'Ivoire, as was demonstrated by his visit to Abidjan in 1957. At the time of the celebrations for Ivorian independence in August 1960, he sent a large delegation and invited Houphouët-Boigny to Accra. At the end of August, Houphouët-Boigny dispatched emissaries to Accra to discuss cooperation. These contacts made a meeting possible between the two leaders on September 19, 1960 at Half-Assini, not far from the village where Nkrumah was born.

This was a memorable event. It was a tight race. No one-upmanship was possible. The differences were numerous and obvious. Neither of the two leaders was inclined to yield. Despite everything, Houphouët seemed to want to listen and perhaps to cooperate. But Nkrumah was incapable of presenting a precise plan of cooperation. Why did he, who was ordinarily so methodical and eager to propose a plan, not feel at ease? The chance for cooperation between pragmatism and idealism was lost. It was a great failure in the pursuit of the dream of unity. Henceforth relations between the two states would decline. Suspicions did not cease to rain down on both sides. On every point, Côte d'Ivoire opposed Ghana's arguments, and Houphouët seemed like one of Nkrumah's fiercest enemies.

To some extent, it was the same with Nigeria, which was by far the most populated country in Africa. Since 1957, Nkrumah's relations with two Nigerian leaders, Awolowo and Balewa, had not been the best, as was indicated in chapter 4. These leaders had a hard time understanding why independent Ghana sought to withdraw from technical and economic organizations that united the countries of British West Africa. At Lagos, the authorities also wondered if Nkrumah was not supporting the movement in east Cameroon that was hostile to the association with Nigeria. The help that Ghana gave to Nigerian dissidents exacerbated relations.

The tension was evident at the time of Nigeria's independence on October 1, 1960. As a Nigerian diplomat declared directly, "either Ghana collaborates with us in Africa, or is against us. Since collaboration implies subordination, Ghana opposes us."[85] In international meetings, often without warning, Nigerians would deplore Nkrumah's ambition and megalomania.

Indeed, the declaration made by the chief of the delegation of Nigeria, Y. M. Sulé, to the second conference of independent states at Addis Ababa in June 1960 is revealing:

> Pan-Africanism is the only solution to our problems in Africa, whatever they are. No one doubts the need to promote pan-Africanism. But we must not be sentimental; we must be realistic. That is why we would like to report that at this time the idea of forming a union of African states is premature, too radical and perhaps overambitious.... Any action to promote cooperation between African countries is good and acceptable. I must warn you, however, that personal ambition for power can spoil everything.... If someone commits the error of feeling that he is the Messiah whose mission is to lead Africa, pan-Africanism will meet a certain defeat. Let us remember what Hitler thought and did in Nazi Germany and what it meant for the entire world.[86]

The tone of this declaration surprised conference attendees and observers. But Sulé frankly expressed what Nigerian leaders felt deep down.

Nkrumah criticized Nigeria in turn. He deplored the "neo-colonialist influences" tolerated by Tafawa Balewa's government. Despite his visit to Lagos, suspicions persisted. The complexity of the Nigerian regime and the political predominance of the conservatives in the North prevented the development of relations between Lagos and Accra. And yet it was difficult to imagine regional regroupment and African unity without Nigeria. In sum, Nkrumah's inability to reassure his neighbors and to formulate a program of practical cooperation with them made his dream uncertain.

Africa was experiencing a lot of diplomatic movement around the end of the year. Politicians were traveling in all directions, each carrying their own ideas, and none of them ready to accept those of another. The issue of regroupment and unity remained the great preoccupation. With the Congo crisis, the political activities become still more intense. Houphouët-Boigny and King Mohammad V of Morocco invited one another to conferences at Brazzaville and Rabat. The first conference made an appeal chiefly to Francophones, the second to heads of state critical of French policy. Africa was divided. In the face of this situation, the issue of reorganization between Ghana, Guinea and Mali took a new turn.

The collapse of the Federation of Mali drew Sékou Touré and Modibo Keïta closer together. In December 1960, they met at Siguiri in Guinea to wipe away the personal animosities and disagreements that arose at the time of the 1958 referendum, and to examine the general situation in Africa. They could not help but criticize the "neo-colonialist spirit" of the conference that Houphouët and his allies called at Brazzaville for mid-December. They also agreed to work in concert with Nkrumah to find a suitable solution to African problems.

Upon their return home, Touré and Keïta informed Nkrumah of their private meeting at Siguiri. Nkrumah was delighted and suggested a meeting for the three of them at Conakry before the Rabat conference in January of 1961. On December 23, 1960, Kwame Nkrumah and Modibo Keïta arrived in the capital of Guinea. The conversations focused on Africa's evolution and on relations between their countries. Thus, on Christmas Eve of 1960, they announced the formation of a union between their three states. It was the union of Ghana, Guinea, and Mali, also known as the Union of African States after the conference of Bamako on June 26, 1961. Given the cooling of relations between Nkrumah and Touré since 1959, one may wonder why they created this new union. Was there a need for a common front against Franco-Ivorian diplomacy and U.N.

threats to the Congo? The crisis in Africa explains the formation of the union.

Whatever the case, the three leaders promised to work for their common independence and for African unity. But, just as in 1958, political unification was only a verbal commitment. The meeting at Conakry was mostly important in terms of foreign policy for the three states. The actual aim of the union was to formulate a common perspective on a certain number of urgent problems, namely moves against the unity of Congo, the war in Algeria, and France's activities which the Brazzaville Conference "hailed" for its work in Africa.

Indeed, Houphouët and the twelve Francophone leaders had yet to demand self-determination for Algeria. Nor did they make a declaration regarding French nuclear installations in the Sahara. By contrast, Ghana, Guinea, and Mali did not hide their opposition to nuclear tests in Africa. Moreover, they had already recognized Algeria's temporary government and desired the immediate independence of Algeria. The three leaders were equally worried about the intensification of the Congo crisis. The secession of Katanga and Kasai, the meteoric rise of Colonel Joseph Désire Mobutu (Sésé Séko), the overthrow of President Joseph Kasavubu and the arrest of Patrice Lumumba—all this seemed to indicate a plot that Nkrumah, Touré and Keïta judged necessary to condemn. At the U.N. in New York, the Brazzaville group supported the delegation of Kasavubu, while the union of Ghana, Guinea and Mali supported the delegation of Lumumba. Despite their agreement in broad strokes, Nkrumah and his allies were incapable of ironing out their differences regarding the Congo.

After Casablanca, the leaders of the union tried to develop the technical aspects of their agreement. From January 9-16, 1961 in Accra, the delegates discussed the plan for a common currency and for a common bank of issue as well as other forms of relevant cooperation. Guinea, which had its own currency, desired the creation of one monetary zone shared between the three. The minister of finance, Gbedemah, vehemently opposed it once again, and Mali could not yet make up its mind about whether it would remain in the Franc Zone.

According to Ghanaian sources, the only form of fiscal coopera-tion between the three states came down to the transfer of Ghanaian aid to Mali via Conakry. This transaction of exchange enabled the Central Bank of Guinea to transfer some of the equivalent amount in CFA francs to Bamako and thus to free itself from the French cur-rency. Experts' discussions in Accra did not help the union advance towards political integration. Moreover, relations (especially between Accra and Conakry) seemed to turn sour. As a result, Nkrumah was absent from the festivities for Sékou Touré's inauguration in 1961.

Despite its inadequacies, the Ghana-Guinea-Mali Union aroused a great deal of interest everywhere among the African elite for the supposedly anti-colonialist and revolutionary character of its leaders. The absence of tangible and permanent functional structures would prevent it from realizing the dream of unity. In this respect, it is nec-essary to recognize that Nkrumah was still far from approaching his goal. If at the regional level the results seemed negligible, what could one hope for at the continental level where differences were even more marked?

Whatever the result, the dream of unity offered Nkrumah a di-rection in life. This dream gave him the heart to move unceasingly from one capital to another, distribute Ghanaian funds generously, maintain dialogue with other leaders and to raise pan-African aware-ness as much among the masses as among the elite.

6

THE CONGO CRISIS AND THE DREAM OF UNITY

Given the importance of the Congo crisis on the African as well as the international scene, it is important to sketch its main features before addressing its impact on the evolution of the subject matters of 'regrouping' and unity. Indeed, the Congo crisis gave Kwame Nkrumah the chance to show his abilities as a mediator in foreign politics. He maintained constant contact with Dag Hammarskjöld, the secretary general of the United Nations (U.N.); Dwight Eisenhower and then John F. Kennedy, the presidents of the United States; Nikita Khrushchev, leader of the Soviet Union, and other foreign heads of state. To a great extent, the future of the dream of African unity played itself out in the Congo.

*President John F. Kennedy meets with the President of the Republic
of Ghana, Osagyefo Dr. Kwame Nkrumah, ca. 1961 (Abbie Rowe.
White House Photographs. John F. Kennedy Presidential Library
and Museum, Boston).*

From the first day of its independence on June 30, 1960 to the end
of the secession of Katanga in January 1963, Congo was at the center
of diplomatic activities in Africa. The U.N. Security Council and the
General Assembly dedicated many sessions to it, in which the positions of Moscow and Washington faced off, as well as the positions
advanced by African countries from the Brazzaville and Casablanca
groups. The Soviet bloc and Nkrumah supported Lumumba and the
legitimate government, while the West and moderate African states
favored Kasavubu.

The Congo crisis was also an imbroglio that seriously affected
Kwame Nkrumah's image. For him, contacts with the great powers
were signs of importance. These relations seemed to prove the accuracy of his doctrine whereby a "small country" could play a de-
terminative role on the international scene. Thus, the ability of the
Ghanaian contingent to disarm Congolese troops and to reestablish

order at Leopoldville would be a success in which Nkrumah could delight and one that would increase his prestige. Cooperation with the U.N., influence on Lumumba and the active presence of Ghanaians on the ground made him still more optimistic.

But would it be the same when Congo transformed into a battlefield between Kennedy and Khrushchev? And what would happen when, out of exasperation at the behavior of General Henry Alexander and Colonel Joseph Ankrah, Lumumba turned to Sékou Touré and the Soviets who urged him to invade Katanga with the Congolese army and to distrust the U.N.? These considerations already heralded the challenges that would entangle the Ghanaian ambassadors, Andrew Dijn and Nathaniel Welbeck.

THE CRISIS IN CONGO

The Congo crisis should be understood in light of various factors, including Belgium's colonial policy, the fierce opposition between African nationalists, and intervention by the U.N. and foreign powers. The increasingly ruthless struggle between Joseph Kasavubu, Patrice Lumumba, Moïse Tshombe and Joseph Désire Mobutu (Sésé Séko), their alliances and their reversals reveal the political mire of the Congo soon after its independence. This was the crisis that Nkrumah aspired to arbitrate and resolve with the assistance of the U.N. in accordance with his vision of African unity. As he later came to recognize, Congo was a challenge.[87]

Since the Congo crisis appeared to be a principally African affair, Nkrumah, abiding by his pan-African doctrine, took the initiative of creating consensus in Africa. On July 12, 1960, he promptly sent a telegram to other heads of state informing them of his decision to dispatch a special fact-finding mission to Leopoldville. He thought that the gravity of the situation and his direct relations with Congolese leaders demanded this step. Once again, many heads of state badly tolerated this initiative and did not plan to renounce their prerogatives to the benefit of Ghanaian diplomacy. Like so many others, President Tubman was really vexed.

Indeed, just like Nkrumah, each leader dreamed of expanding his influence in the Congo and, beyond that, of establishing his image on the international scene. For each, the Congo crisis was a chance to prove himself. But it was also a source of division. Hostility between the moderate leaders of the Brazzaville or Monrovia group and those of the Casablanca group tarnished the prospect of unity. Nkrumah lost many "friends" in the Congo without persuading his adversaries in return. In the opinion of all, he emerged from it weakened and even isolated, his dream of African unity having suffered a terrible blow.

A few words about the origin of the conflict helps to better elucidate its significance. It all began with Belgian colonialism. Maintaining complete colonial power, Belgium did not introduce a single reform to prepare Congo for independence. Moreover, the very word "independence" was inconceivable and unacceptable among Belgian administrators and settlers in central Africa.

For a long time, Africans did not possess freedoms of press or association or the right to a travel passport. Despite the expansion of Christianity, they did not have access to higher education. The country lacked a modern elite. The Belgian colonial system was a regime of intensified exploitation and paternalism that refused to believe in the maturity of its subjects.

Beginning from 1950, as part of the wave of political unrest that shook neighboring territories under French control, African townspeople began to form political movements, at first mostly based on ethnic criteria. This was how the Alliance of the Bakongo (Abako) was created in 1950 under the leadership of Kasavubu. At its inception, this movement defined itself as an association of mutual aid and cultural renaissance comprised of members of the Kongo ethnic group which occupied the region of Leopoldville. Little by little, it took the form of a political movement and thus drew townspeople from other regions. Abako therefore has the distinction of being the first Congolese organization to mobilize African youth for political action. In 1957, at the first municipal elections ever organized in Congo, the party won in "the City," the vast African neighborhood of Leopoldville (Kinshasa).

In 1958 ethnic and political organizations multiplied within the country. For example, a businessman from Elisabethville (Lubumbashi), Moïse Tshombe, organized the *Confédération des associations du Katanga* (Conakat). In 1960 Conakat would go on to join with the Katanga union, an extreme right party of Belgian settlers. The creation of the *Mouvement National Congolais* (MNC) by Lumumba in October 1958 was something new. The MNC distinguished itself as a genuine party which straightaway gave itself a national mission and drew members from all social and ethnic layers. The crisis that broke out after independence and that captured Nkrumah's attention day after day placed all these movements in opposition, with their leaders often reacting in unpredictable and ruthless ways.

Very early in his political career, Nkrumah was interested in the Congo, a choice region because of its strategic position, wealth, demographic power, and the intellectual curiosity of its leaders. At the start, as was appropriate, he supported the "doyen" of the Congolese nationalists, Kasavubu, who reigned in the province of Leopoldville (Kinshasa). He had been invited to the first conference of African peoples at Accra in December 1958, but he could not attend. Lumumba, however, did participate and benefited by meeting Nkrumah through their common acquaintance, Ehud Avriel, the very influential ambassador from Israel. In adding a pan-African dimension to his Congolese nationalism, Lumumba reinforced his image as a leader called upon to play a great role on the Congolese stage.

In other words, the diplomatic opposition marking the African world at the end of 1960 was already emerging. Since his reputation continued growing, Lumumba little by little replaced Kasavubu's influence in Accra. In this way, he became the favored ally of Kwame Nkrumah. The Ghanaian leader thought Lumumba's MNC would prevail over other parties and would direct the new republic of Congo. Therefore, Ghana was ready to grant him the support he needed.

Under these conditions, Kasavubu turned increasingly to his ethnic and religious brother, Abbot Fulbert Youlou, president of the council of the government of Congo-Brazzaville, to fill the void created around him. The rapprochement between Kasavubu and

Youlou on the one hand and between Lumumba and Nkrumah on the other corresponded to the differences that caused the countries of the Brazzaville group and the Casablanca group to face off.

How had they reached this point so soon in the Congo? As if to prove the unpredictability of history, two significant events succeeding one another in the week of December 28, 1958 to January 4, 1959 sparked the powder keg. First, Belgian authorities allowed Lumumba to hold a popular meeting on Sunday, December 28, after his return from the pan-African conference at Accra. The second event was the riot of Sunday, January 4, 1959, that broke out after the prohibition of the Abako meeting.

According to Yves Bénot, "there was a mob" at the meeting convened in the black quarter of Leopoldville by Lumumba upon his return from Accra.[88] The audience, which numbered around 10,000, bubbled over with enthusiasm when the speaker denounced the plan to divide Congo and urged the people to win their own independence in unity. This meeting was a resounding call for a "mass political action, as there had been in the countries of western Africa, those that had just secured independence and those that soon would."[89] Undeniably the Accra pan-African conference fermented awareness in the colonized peoples of central Africa. This delighted Nkrumah, as he remarked in his book on the Congo.[90]

In turn, a week later, Abako called the people to a public meeting on Sunday, January 4, 1959. To their surprise, the meeting was banned. Inexplicably, news of the prohibition was not made public until the morning of the conference. With good reason, Yves Bénot has insisted that at this moment, "the man to bring down, in the eyes of the colonizer, was Kasavubu before all others, the one who first dared to speak of immediate emancipation."[91]

On this day, in the Kalama quarter of "the City," a great crowd gathered, eager to hear their leader. Much to their surprise they learned that the conference had been canceled. Angry, they refused to disperse, despite the pleas of Kasavubu and his lieutenants. The presence of security forces further incensed the thousands of politically concerned men and women. A veritable human tide from the black ghetto, a crowd enlarged by a group of young people returning from the stadium, was growing impatient, agitated and restless. They walked over the circular boulevard leading to Leopoldville, the white city which was separated from the ghetto by a belt of camps and parks.

Law enforcement responded rapidly. Military and police groups were put on a state of alert and were asked to rein in the movement. Thus, a veritable military operation was unleashed that would last for two weeks. When all the African neighborhoods were finally subdued, there were fifty-nine casualties according to official sources. But the real number seemed to be close to 500. The courts ordered hundreds of arrests as well as search warrants in houses, churches, and offices of political associations. Kasavubu and the other African leaders of the City were all arrested and locked up. Abako was dissolved. Terror reigned in the New Year.

This spontaneous riot resounded like a thunderbolt striking the stupor of Belgian colonial and metropolitan authorities. How could they regain control of the situation? Did they need to organize a formal intervention like the French had done in Algeria? These were the questions being asked in Leopoldville as well as in Brussels. Aware of the limits of Belgium's military ability, King Baudouin and the government decided to meet with Congolese nationalists. At Brussels, they even proclaimed independence for Congo—something that shocked many observers.

Lack of preparation permeated the atmosphere at the round table where Belgians and Congolese discussed Congo's future following January 20, 1960. The meeting also discussed the fundamental law concerning Congo's political structures, which the Belgian government adopted on May 10 and which clarified the nature of the Congolese regime after its independence, and the legislative and provincial elections planned for May 1960.

This race against the clock, which was hardly justified, risked leading Congo to the point of chaos. As further confirmation of the reckless planning, sectarian fervor in Katanga and Kasai were rising and seemed imminent. The victory of Lumumba's party in the elections of May 1960 showed his party to be leading the country with 41 seats out of 137, but it suggested a political situation that was rather unstable and precarious. Everywhere, the latent conflict seemed to become increasingly serious.

Thus, on the eve of independence, four obstacles weighed on Congo's future: 1) the glaring failure of preparations for independence, which recalled the Guinean situation of 1958; 2) the increasingly apparent will to secede on the part of Tshombe and his Belgian allies of Katanga, the heart of the Congolese economy; 3) the strong presence of Belgian administrators in the administration of the territory and the shortage of national executives; and finally, 4) the total absence of an armed force able to maintain order and security. Cumulatively, these obstacles underscore the gravity of the domestic conflict as well as the difficulties of diplomatic maneuvering for Nkrumah and all other foreigners involved in the Congolese drama. Everyone was expecting troubles after independence on June 30, 1960.

As expected, these prophecies were realized. King Baudouin's speech at the independence ceremonies sounded like actual praise of the work of the colonial powers. The tone seemed to be a deliberate provocation. Lumumba responded vehemently. To observers the clash between king and prime minister recalled the oratorical jousts between De Gaulle and Sékou Touré. Above all it presaged difficulties to come.

From July 1, disaster was unleashed everywhere in the country with inexplicable swiftness. As usual, public forces intervened violently. The reappointment of the Belgian general Janssens as commander of the Congolese troops added fuel to the fire. Mutinies broke out in all camps against the presence of Belgian officers in positions of command. Belgian bases were placed in a state of emergency, and European families hastily made way by boat to Brazzaville. It was an exodus; there was panic and general disorder.

On July 11 Katanga proclaimed its independence as expected. Belgian troops based in Congo intervened, assisted by a task force of paratroopers specially sent from Europe. These soldiers bombarded Congolese military installations as well as the residential districts of many cities. They helped to retake the international airport of Leopoldville, which had been seized by Congolese soldiers.

These events resulted in reactions of horror and disapproval throughout the world. In many capitals in Africa and abroad, demonstrations of solidarity with the government of Congo were organized. Thus, Congo aroused the awareness of the world's progressives, and Lumumba seemed like one of the great figures in the anti-colonial movement.

In the face of the gravity of the crisis, the Congolese government made an appeal to the U.N. on July 11. The same day, Nkrumah communicated with Lumumba and promised to help him. He immediately sent a battalion from the Ghanaian army as contingent forces for the U.N. Soon, there were approximately 2,500 Ghanaian soldiers in the Congo, in addition to doctors, administrative executives, and military corps engineers (a union pact, signed secretly on August 8, 1960, would reinforce ties between Ghana and the Congo).

If Nkrumah's reaction was immediate and rapid, that of the United States was equally so. American military cargo planes transported much of the contingent forces to Leopoldville. Better yet the American consulate at Leopoldville was following Congo's development long before independence. In this respect, Thomas Kanza was right when he insisted that relations already existed between the Americans and the Abako of Kasavubu.[92]

In June 1960, President Eisenhower and his secretary of state, Foster Dulles, perfectly grasped the scope of the Congo affair. Their policy came down to preventing by any means the penetration of Soviet influence in central Africa. And so, they placed on the ground at Leopoldville a team of knowledgeable and fast acting agents. The team was led by Ambassador Clare Timberlake, who had African experience, and including Lawrence Devlin, bureau chief of the CIA, who already knew Mobutu. In this way, Washington marked its presence in the Congo. The fortnight of catastrophe, of which Yves Bénot spoke, and other subsequent events, can be understood in light of the tacit rivalry between the United States and other countries, including Nkrumah's Ghana.

The crisis reached its peak between September and December of 1960. In the beginning of September, the national army of the Congo, which still depended on Lumumba, was victorious in Kasai and with great popular support threw itself into conquering Katanga. Neither Ambassador Timberlake nor Andrew Cordier, the principal assistant of the general secretary of the U.N. for Congolese affairs, was in favor of this offensive. So, they intervened with the secretariat of President Kasavubu to halt it, although they were aware of the constitutional limits set on presidential power. According to many observers, the pressure that these diplomats exerted on the Congolese president was a crucial factor in the new confusion that erupted in the Congo.

Consequently, on September 5, Kasavubu dismissed Lumumba from the post of prime minister as well as all the other members of government who belonged to his party. In the opinion of many experts in constitutional law, this unlawful decision was tantamount to a *coup d'état*. Lumumba in turn dismissed Kasavubu from the presidency. It was anarchy, pure and simple. Two days later, the parliament re-established Lumumba as head of the legitimate government. But, unexpectedly, U.N. forces at Leopoldville, in agreement with western powers that no longer trusted Lumumba, confirmed their about-face in a shocking way.

For some time, there had been a decline in cooperation between the representative of the secretary general of the U.N. in Congo, Ralph Bunche, and the Ghanaian ambassador, Andrew Djin, which had originally permitted the re-establishment of law and order. The new representative of the U.N., Rajeshwar Dayal, and his colleague, Andrew Cordier, sought a solution in line with the ideas of Dag Hammarskjöld. However, Hammarskjöld and Lumumba did not agree over the interpretation of the charter overseeing the deployment of U.N. forces. In candid language, the prime minister scolded the general secretary for the initiatives that he took without consulting the Congolese government, as well as for the dispatch of Irish and Swedish contingents in Katanga instead of African forces.[93]

For his part, Hammarskjöld seemed paternalistic and biased, and had a hard time accepting Lumumba's revolutionary character and his affiliation with Nkrumah. He considered Lumumba the main cause of Congo's ailments and was not inclined to make the task easier for him. In a demonstration of this hostility, Hammarskjöld refused to bring the Congolese delegation along in his plane to New York.[94]

Given the opposition of the secretary general and his men to the Congolese army's military offensive against Katanga, U.N. forces directly interfered in Congo's domestic affairs. They openly criticized the head of the government even though it was he who had made the appeal for their intervention. They guarded the Leopoldville airport to control the movement of Lumumba and his men. In addition, they prevented the prime minister from having access to a telephone or radio and thus from mobilizing the people, while Kasavubu and Tshombe were leading a virulent campaign against Lumumba on Radio-Brazzaville and Radio-Elisabethville.

In a telegram addressed to Dag Hammarskjöld, Nkrumah responded to this betrayal and unforeseen interference. He threatened to withdraw the Ghanaian contingent and to place it at the disposal of the legitimate government.[95] Not long after, before the general assembly of the U.N. in New York, Nkrumah denounced neo-colonialist maneuvers in the Congo and proposed an African solution for the conflict to guarantee Congo's independence. But matters were not so simple. The interference of the U.N. and of the great powers made the idea impracticable.

Strengthened by the support of western countries and moderate African countries, Kasavubu adjourned parliament on September 14 with the complicity of Mobutu, commander of the Congolese troops. In the opinion of all observers, this crucial event marked Mobutu's first *coup d'état.*

For, in the final analysis, it was the colonel who henceforth controlled power. Kasavubu distanced Lumumba, and Mobutu "neutralized" Kasavubu. This was the game. Through general commissaries whom he appointed and who acted as true ministers, the colonel effectively led the Congo.

Congolese soldiers loyal to Mobutu occupied Leopoldville. Lumumba was placed under house arrest. At the U.N. in New York, the delegation representing the Kasavubu government received investiture. It was a great defeat for Nkrumah, his allies and above all Patrice Lumumba.

On November 27, 1960, Lumumba escaped with two companions in the direction of Stanleyville, where Antoine Gizenga was in the process of re-establishing the legitimate government in his name. But the fugitives were arrested in Kasai, despite the presence of Ghanaian troops then operating in the region. Catherine Hoskyns thought that this arrest, and the eventual assassination, could have been prevented if the Ghanaian officers had remained faithful to a pro-Lumumba policy.[96] Lumumba and his two companions were taken away as prisoners to the capital on December 1. It was there, at Camp Hardy near Thysville not far from the capital, according to the description of Yves Bénot, where Lumumba's great suffering began.

Indeed, according to the sources, the order to kill Lumumba had already been approved by President Eisenhower at the time of the National Security Council meeting on August 18, 1960 in Washington, D.C.[97] The situation was critical. Aware of the difficulties of his Congolese policy, Nkrumah tried in vain to reconcile Lumumba and Kasavubu. He also proposed the organization of a unified military command of African forces in the Congo to the leaders who participated in the first conference of independent states in 1958. But the Ghanaian diplomats and government staff at Leopoldville no longer inspired trust.

The Congo affair was critical on another level as well. In addition to the exorbitant cost of the operation that opposition parliamentarians at Accra denounced, the events highlighted a lack of coordination among Nkrumah's representatives at Leopoldville. The Congolese capital became a meeting ground for great dignitaries, each one bringing his own opinion and anxious to communicate it to President Nkrumah. For the ambassador and other authorized diplomats in the Congo, the ignorance of the French was a definite handicap.

Several problems threatened the success of Nkrumah's policy. In the first place, Ghana seemed to not have the men that it needed in the Congo at this critical moment. The diplomats who served there were named because of their political experience in the country rather than their competence in foreign policy. For instance, the ambassadors Andrew Djin and Nathaniel Welbeck were among the first officeholders of the CPP, but they poorly understood the tortuous and slippery world of international relations. Neither of them benefited from the kind of training for which the Ghanaian diplomats at the U.N. were famous, for example. As for the military command, officers for the most part did not share Nkrumah's political orientation. To complicate matters still, General Alexander, who was English, often had trouble with his black Ghanaian officers. In sum, from very early on, many observers questioned the loyalty of such a task force.

Secondly, Nkrumah's policy suffered from the tacit opposition between the Ghanaian ambassador and the government staff. Ambassador Djin, who should have recognized the international character of the Ghanaian armed forces, could not understand why the officers of his country refused to execute his orders. No cooperation was possible between the chief diplomat and the commander-in-chief of the troops. How could Nkrumah's policy succeed in such conditions? The arrival of a new ambassador, Nathaniel Welbeck, whom Sékou Touré had dismissed from Conakry, did not lead to better political coordination between diplomats and officers.

Finally, the Congolese themselves had trouble explaining the choice of an Englishman at the head of the strongest African contingent. For them, the presence of General Alexander and of other English officers in the Ghanaian contingent went against the doctrine of Africanization advocated by Nkrumah. Some could thus explain the role that Ghanaians played in the weakening of Lumumba's power.

Paradoxically, the Ghanaian officers displayed their increasing opposition to Lumumba. For example, according to Anicet Kashamura, former Congo minister of information, Colonel Ankrah, the highest ranking black officer in the Ghanaian contingent at Leopoldville, permitted himself the following remark about the prime minister: "A government that can no longer control the situation no longer has its *raison d'être*."[98] A fine justification for a *coup d'état!* Consequently, no one was surprised that Ghanaian forces prevented Lumumba from using the media.

Lumumba directly addressed Nkrumah to complain about this unfortunate situation. In reply, he received a long, rather terse, paternalistic, and disappointing letter. Nkrumah advised him to collaborate with his enemies, even the fiercest, as well as with the U.N. for "tactical" reasons, and to put his trust in him. It was a strange thing for the Ghanaian president, who seems to have been known for his modesty, to give lessons to the Congolese leader and to boast about his own expertise on the international scene.[99] In fact, one might wonder if Nkrumah was familiar with the files himself or if his ambassador informed him of events transpiring in the Congo. It seems that the reports that were delivered to him had been written much more to please him than to describe the actual situation. Whatever the case, he appeared to be ignorant of what was currently taking place in the Congo: Lumumba no longer held power.

The blunders of Ambassador Nathaniel Welbeck further complicated the situation for Nkrumah. At the beginning of October, Kasavubu declared him *persona non-grata* because of his participation in rallies and other demonstrations of the MNC. Nkrumah, however, refused to recall him immediately. Consequently, an overnight battle opposed Congolese soldiers and the U.N. forces responsible for guarding the ambassador's residence. In the end, he reached Accra under the protection of General Alexander.

For a long time after this date, although diplomatic relations were maintained, Ghana would have no ambassador in the Congo. This result was far different from what Nkrumah had hoped for. His Congo policy ended in disaster. Could he reinvigorate it through his African diplomacy? To help the government of Gizenga, which was solidly established at Stanleyville, and to counteract the conference of Francophone African states where Kasavubu and Tshombe were expected to participate in Brazzaville on December 15-18, 1960, Nkrumah and his allies planned a conference in Casablanca on January 5-7, 1961.

As emerges from the preceding discussion, the Congo was at the center of African diplomacy. Increasingly, it was the source of the rapprochement that was unfolding between some African countries and foreign powers, as well as the increasing hostility manifesting between the heads of state. It was also at the source of the regional regroupment with which the different countries identified.

The success of Kwame Nkrumah's dream would depend on the outcome of this crisis: a crisis, it should be noted, in which many protagonists were hoping to find Nkrumah's diplomacy unsuccessful. At this point it is appropriate to return to the Ghana-Guinea-Mali Union and the conference of Rabat-Casablanca.

CASABLANCA OR TRANS-SAHARAN REGROUPMENT

At the beginning of 1961, a divided Africa was facing a crisis. More than ever, Kwame Nkrumah was haunted by the Congo and by his dream of unity. For him the weakness of states and their inability to bring about an African solution demanded unity.

Other leaders also shared this preoccupation with regroupment. The interference of the great powers in African affairs, the risk of a nuclear accident in the Sahara and Lumumba's arrest were also sources of concern that explain why Nkrumah and his allies participated in the Rabat conference. Not only did the monarch of Morocco condemn the role that the U.N., the great powers and the countries of the Brazzaville group played in the Congo, but he also sought allies to support his ambitions concerning Mauritania. In sum, for Mohammed V and Nkrumah, there were plenty of reasons to broaden the scope of the Ghana-Guinea-Mali Union.

The king inaugurated the conference on January 5, 1961 with the participation of presidents Kwame Nkrumah, Sékou Touré, Modibo Keïta and Gamal Abdel Nasser; the personal representative of King Idris I of Libya; the president of the provisional government of Algeria, Ferhat Abbas; and an observer sent by the government of Ceylon (Sri Lanka). No Francophone country of the Brazzaville group was invited. Ethiopia, Liberia, Togo, Somalia, and Sudan declined their invitations. For three days, the leaders and their specialized ministers painted a picture of the overall situation of the continent and discussed means for remedying the crisis.

As should be expected, Congolese affairs took up a fair part of the discussions. The continuing participation of African countries in U.N. forces led to a tense debate among the heads of state. Sékou Touré, Modibo Keïta, Mohammed V and Nasser pressured Nkrumah intensely to revise his policy toward the U.N. These leaders were ready to withdraw their contingents from Congo because of the hostility of the U.N. forces towards the Lumumba-Gizenga government. Despite his support for this government, Nkrumah believed that the U.N. forces were a guarantee of order and stability and therefore did not want to dismantle them.

In the final communiqué, the heads of state reserved the right to withdraw their contingents from U.N. forces if U.N. forces did not respect their mission. All but Nkrumah would go on to recall their forces confirming the lack of unity within the Casablanca group.

Despite everything, the Rabat conference represented progress in the quest for unity as far as it established a political regroupment that went beyond the regional framework of the Ghana-Guinea-Mali Union. The attempt seemed like that of trans-Saharan regroupment. In the wake of the conference, the Ghana-Guinea-Mali Union, without disappearing from the political scene, yielded to the new regroupment by functioning within the context of the Casablanca group. The heads of state felt united because of their radical opposition to colonialism and their desire to build Africa on the base of institutions that were more "revolutionary" than those of their Brazzaville peers.

The resolutions of the conference revealed a consensus regarding the Congo crisis, France's nuclear tests in the Sahara, aid to Gizenga's government, Algerian independence, and the necessity for inter-African cooperation. They appear in the document known as the "Charter of Casablanca." This document does not address the issue of unity as Nkrumah envisioned it. However, in order to promote unity and security, it recommended the establishment of a certain number of unifying organizations, namely, an African consulting assembly composed of representatives of each state and four inter-

African committees responsible for political, economic, cultural, and military affairs.

The political committee, made up of heads of states or their authorized representatives, was called upon to gather at regular intervals to coordinate the overall policy of member states. Though an executive organization, this committee was not the federal government that Nkrumah recommended they create. Far from restricting itself to the technical cooperation characteristic of Brazzaville group countries, the signatories of the charter of Casablanca seemed to understand the necessity for a gradual movement toward governmental unity. That said, the political committee never got off the ground.

Neither Nkrumah nor Touré attended the conference of heads of state in Cairo in August 1961; the meetings planned for March and October 1962 were also cancelled, as well as those for December 1962 and May 1963. Nkrumah, Touré and Keïta held discussions in Accra in April of 1961 and in Bamako in June. They refused to participate in the conference of African states in Monrovia. However, the lack of a concrete program, in addition to their shared opposition to external adversaries, explains the postponements. In brief, each leader retained his autonomy.

By contrast, the economic committee did meet on several occasions and addressed the issue of an African common market. As such, customs' tariffs were reduced between signatory states, and the organization of commercial trade shows were made easier. A postal union was created, and air transportation provider collaboration was strengthened among the different countries. The events in Congo in general and Lumumba's transfer to and death in Elisabethville led to the creation of a unified military command; the military forces of the signatory states were called upon to assure the defense of the countries against foreign aggression.

From the point of view of foreign policy, changes of great significance would take place. Due to pressure from Nasser, Nkrumah began to change his relations with Israel and to support the Palestinian cause. The events in Congo, the CIA's role in Lumumba's death and the increasingly socialist orientation of his ideology would also aggravate his relations with the United States, Great Britain, and other western countries to the benefit of those in the Soviet bloc. The unforeseen result presented a paradox, since Nkrumah's original Congolese policy aimed at keeping Africa out of the Cold War.

From 1961 onward, competition between Americans and Soviets turned out to be an increasingly important factor in foreign policy in Africa. While keeping his independence, Nkrumah seemed increasingly suspect in Washington and London. Africa's moderate leaders did not conceal their hostility toward him because of his attitudes and the aid that he continued to give to dissidents. Consequently, his image was tarnished in certain circles, and his dream of unity became problematic.

Eventually, political and economic difficulties encouraged subversive movements against Nkrumah. Disillusioned officers and political leaders began to talk to and receive aid from the CIA and other Western agents. While awaiting the outcome of these plots, it must be reemphasized that the Congo crisis was a crucial point in Nkrumah's life. It demonstrated on the open stage the drama of Africa's lack of unity, her weakness at the level of leadership and statecraft. The crisis also reinforced the strong visibility of the United States and other foreign countries. Washington managed to impose its solution; and unlike his totem, the crow, Nkrumah could not fly away to avoid the aftermath of the Congo conflict.[100] The dream could not take flight; it had lost its wings and the dreamer had lost his mystique.

The formation of the Casablanca group demanded that the countries of the Brazzaville group enlarge their scope beyond the Francophone zone. The opposition of Nigeria, Ethiopia and Liberia to Ghana's politics made this counter action easier. Thus, the conference of African and Madagascan heads of state took place in Monrovia from May 8-12, 1961. In addition to Francophone heads of state and the host, Liberia, attendees included presidents or heads of government from Nigeria, Sierra Leone, Togo, Somalia, Tunisia, Ethiopia, and Libya.

Henceforth, from 1961 to 1963, the fundamental problem in Africa was to find common ground between the two groups whose members, while criticizing one another, sensed the imperative for peace and unity. Therefore, Nkrumah and his partners on one side and Tafawa Balewa, Houphouët-Boigny and Haile Selassie and their partners on the other positioned themselves with the goal of establishing dialogue in Africa. To a certain extent, the interstate conference organized at Addis Ababa in May 1963 was an answer to this aspiration.

7

THE OAU AND THE DREAM OF UNITY

From the Conference of Casablanca in January 1961 to the end of the secession in Katanga in January 1963, President Nkrumah pursued his quest for unity. His task became increasingly complex because of difficulties with the leaders of Togo, Côte d'Ivoire, Nigeria, and other neighboring countries. The tension in the sub-region affected Nkrumah's image and his policy of unification.

Since 1957, when British Togo merged with Ghana by referendum, the leaders of the former French mandate of Togo had feared Nkrumah's "expansionist aims." A. K. Barden, John Tettegah and other members of the Bureau of African Affairs did show their hostility to the leader of Togolese independence, Sylvanus Olympio. Yet, Olympio and Nkrumah held candid and cordial discussions for a little while. As a precaution to affirm his position against Ghana, Olympio established solid relations with Côte d'Ivoire, Guinea, and the Francophone countries. He also counted on an alliance with Nigeria, whose leaders, for their part, also suspected Ghana of interfering in their domestic affairs.

From 1960, when Olympio escaped an attempt on his life, relations between Accra and Lomé took a bad turn. The decrease in cocoa price in Ghana and the resulting smuggling of part of the product on the Togolese market incited tension and finally crisis. The Bureau of African Affairs intensified its radio propaganda against Togo. Some thought that it was encouraging and funding subversive movements against Lomé.

Olympio asked for the implementation of the military pact that had been signed with France. He obtained the help of Houphouët-Boigny, who also complained about Ghana's "connection" to the affairs of the Sanwi on the border. Thus, at the Conference of Lagos in January 1962, members of the Monrovia group threatened to break ties with Ghana if it attacked Togo.

In contrast, Nkrumah seemed to have more success with the Upper Volta (Burkina Faso), his northern neighbor. In 1962, in a gesture of rapprochement, he promised to come to the aid of President Maurice Yaméogo whose government had encountered a serious budget crisis. In August 1962, after the CPP's conference at Kumase, Nkrumah spent a few days in the Northwest of Ghana before beginning an official visit to the Upper Volta. Then came a surprise.

Unforeseen by all, Nkrumah was wounded in a grenade attack in the village of Kulugungu.[101] The borders were immediately closed; the diplomatic opening, which had only just begun, was deferred. Yaméogo then turned back to Houphouët-Boigny. At the same time, he was improving his relations with Sékou Touré on whom he had more than once lavished insults. The trumpet of cooperation sounded in the sub-region—but without Nkrumah.

And in Ghana itself, the opposition wanted to get rid of Nkrumah. Kulugungu was followed by other bomb attacks in Kumase, Accra and even Flagstaff House, the presidential residence. A good number of leaders who were suspected of taking part in the plots put an ocean between themselves and Accra. The government proceeded with many arrests.

But unlike the practices in many other African countries, the guilty had a right to justice. Faithful to the principles of human rights and sensitive of his own penitentiary experience, Nkrumah let justice take its course despite pressures from the party. Even in the opinion of opponents, he did not seem to order any summary execution. Furthermore, the Supreme Court could free defendants! The death in detention of J. B. Danquah, who had urged him to return in 1947, gave rise to bitter criticism in Nigeria and elsewhere. But, according to many observers, this did not taint Nkrumah's steadfast respect of the law and human life.

Whatever the case, Nkrumah lived in fear of conspiracy and assassination. It marked the beginning of his isolation on the national and regional scene.

The assassination of President Sylvanus Olympio on January 13, 1963 sparked rumors concerning the possible role of agents of Accra in the murder. Doubts persisted, even after the confirmation that Togolese soldiers who had recently been demobilized from the French army were responsible. For, unlike other countries, Ghana did not lament the death of the Togolese leader. By contrast, as if to distance itself with Accra, Guinea celebrated the memory of the deceased as one of the modern heroes of Africa.[102]

Accra's daily paper *Evening News* lashed out violently against Sékou Touré whom it nicknamed "the shooting star" and against the "reactionary" Tafawa Balewa for their statements honoring Olympio.[103] With these events, relations between Nkrumah and Touré deteriorated. The countries of the Monrovia group decided to investigate Olympio's murder with the hope of further discrediting Nkrumah. Ghana was increasingly sidelined.

The Togolese crisis thus brought into the same camp leaders who had until recently opposed one another on the African scene. On both sides, they aspired to create more favorable grounds for peace and security. Thus, in mid-February, presidents Houphouët-Boigny, Modibo Keïta and Sékou Touré met and affirmed their opposition to acts of subversion and interference in the domestic affairs of other states. It was a thinly-veiled attack on Ghanaian policy. Nkrumah was losing his allies in western Africa. Tubman and Balewa were delighted.

Certain members of the Casablanca group wanted to nurture better relations with their peers from the Monrovia group. The signing of the Évian Accords, which put an end to the war in Algeria in 1962, facilitated this step. The desire to improve relations was particularly true of Sékou Touré, who already had a bitter experience of political isolation. And so, Guineans warmly welcomed President

Houphouët-Boigny in August of 1962. At Conakry, Houphouët-Boigny, who attached in his own way great importance to both his old friendship with Touré and interstate relations, asked for a meeting between the Monrovia and Casablanca groups, "with the aim of discussing, among brothers, the future of our beloved Africa."[104] Sékou Touré shared this point of view.

As further confirmation of this opinion, the Guinean president declared two months later to the U.N. General Assembly in New York: "African unity does not imply the existence of uniform institutions or executive branches for our states; still less does it mean the creation of a sole party or a sole super-state for the whole of the continent."[105] It was largely understood that he was addressing Nkrumah. Guinea was ready to abandon the Ghana-Guinea-Mali Union for a much broader cooperation at the continental level.

In March of 1963, rumor of the participation of the Ghanaian ambassador at Abidjan, J. K. Quashie, in a plot against Houphouët-Boigny renewed tension. To avoid the awkward situation and mitigate the crisis, Nkrumah recalled his diplomat. Moreover, the other leaders consulted with one another to put an end to the subversion. The way was open for the interstate meeting in Addis Ababa to which all the heads of state were invited.

Before looking at the creation of the Organization of African Unity (OAU), it is necessary to see the result of the politics of the quest for unity up to 1963. As the two preceding chapters have shown, the move to independence in Africa was followed by the division of states into two antagonistic groups on political, ideological, and even personal lines. This accounts in part for the difficulties of Nkrumah's African policy. Despite the dangers of psychological analysis, it could be said that his diplomacy suffered greatly from the enmity his peers felt towards him. However, the pitfalls appeared not to discourage Nkrumah in his dream, which seemed to him more than ever the condition *sine qua non* of independence and progress in Africa.

In the 1960s, all the heads of state spoke of unity. The context demanded it. The reality, however, was different. As emerges from our analysis, the words were on their lips, but not in their hearts. Overall, African leaders preferred to cooperate at the interstate level than to abandon sovereignty in favor of a continental government. As Maurice Glélé-Ahanhanzo observed, they jealously guarded the independence of their countries.[106]

In addition, these leaders were especially obsessed with their own powers and prerogatives as supreme magistrates. In their eyes, as Sékou Touré suggested above or Y. M. Sulé, head of the Nigerian delegation at the second conference of independent states at Addis Ababa in June 1960, the idea of a federal African government was premature and impractical. It was human for each to dream of remaining king in his own domain.

These attitudes stemmed from the conditions in which the states entered independence. As the examples of the former French countries in West Africa (AOF) and Equatorial Africa (AEF) show, independence was attained in the territorial context. The former colonial power influenced the process of transferring power.

It is well known that the referendum of 1958, if not the entire program of French decolonization, was hostile to the federations. The leaders of the former mother countries would have thus engendered distrust on the part of African nationalists toward integration and unity. This attitude is reflected in the approach of the countries involved in the Brazzaville and Monrovia groups. The desire for unity was present, but the will was absent.

Consideration of this point should aid in understanding the weaknesses in Nkrumah's attempts at regional union. For example, for Touré and the other ally, the union of Ghana, Guinea and Mali did not at all aim to create mechanisms for a unified government. Despite their statements, the co-signatories of the union did not stray from their attachment to the sovereignty of their respective countries. What interested them above all was Ghana's material or political aid, followed by cooperation without yielding the rights of sovereignty. In sum, the differences between the men of Casablanca and Monrovia were expressed in what kind of society to build and attitudes toward western powers. Yet, few heads of state were resolved to abandon all for Africa.

In this regard, Nkrumah seemed different. Despite errors in executing his policy, his speech and actions confirm his faith in unity, and so in Africa. Unlike his counterparts, he placed the independence and resources of his country at the service of unity. Thus, it proved to be a difficult struggle between his vision and that of the other leaders present at the great conference in Addis Ababa, on May 15, 1963.

NKRUMAH AND THE CREATION OF THE OAU

On the heights of the Ethiopian capital, 32 African heads of state and government met to discuss Africa and provide it with a continental organization. Only King Hassan II of Morocco, who had just succeeded his father, and President Nicolas Grunitzky of Togo were absent. The crucial and historically important stakes corresponded to the wishes of the population as well as to a certain doctrine about the pan-African dream.

The question that Africans from all sides unceasingly asked themselves was whether their leaders were capable of surmounting their differences and of acting for the higher good of the continent. Given the occasion's importance, each leader did his best to present his best image for posterity. As a result, rhetoric rained down over the hills of Addis Ababa in this infamous week. But since politics could not limit itself to words, closed door working sessions at the conference turned out to be a dramatic battlefield between the two opposing visions of Africa's future.

As was customary, the conference began at the ministerial level. Surrounded by their experts, the ministers of foreign affairs had the task of examining the different proposals regarding the institutionalization of African unity and of presenting their reports to the heads of state. Taking immediate advantage of its role as host and its preconference collection of country proposals, the Ethiopian delegation put forth the idea of an organization of African states with a precise charter and a permanent general secretariat responsible for the organization's actions.

Emperor Haile Selassie had conceived this plan some years before. He had presented it to Kwame Nkrumah during his visit to Accra in

December 1960. The proposal seemed acceptable to the representatives of many countries, but was contradictory to the argument for a federal African government, which Ghanaian diplomacy had worked towards since 1958.

President Kwame Nkrumah and Emperor Haile Selassie, ca. 1963.

It is important to examine the implications of the Ethiopian proposal. To create his plan, Haile Selassie considered several models. The example of the U.N. would be relevant if the Security Council's right of veto belonging to its five permanent members did not appear like a quasi-executive organization. This model was inappropriate in the African context, given the need to respect the principle of equality between states. The organization of American states and even the Arab League were more appropriate sources of inspiration.

The model of the American states impressed the emperor, and everything indicated that he sought to impose it on his guests. Rumors circulated that Ethiopia had engaged the help of Chilean experts in constitutional law to write up his document. This model did not prescribe the creation of a federal or even confederal government. Respectful of the absolute sovereignty of each member state, it required nothing other than consultation and cooperation on issues that met the general approval of the heads of state. In the eyes of the Ethiopians, the model had to be acceptable to all those who dreamed of an African organization as a mechanism for consultation. Other delegations tried to make their proposals prevail, but without success. The ministers could not come to an understanding. Perhaps, the Ghanaian model could obtain the majority.

Led by the minister of foreign affairs, Kojo Botsio, the Ghanaian delegation numbering more than fifty, noisily marked its arrival in Addis Ababa on May 13. From the moment of arrival on the city streets, it began distributing special copies of articles appearing in the newspaper of the CPP, *Spark*, that pertained to imperialism and African unity. Next, at the conference itself, Ghanaians distributed recently published copies of the edition of Nkrumah's most appropriate work, *Africa Must Unite*. An ideological handbook, it contained the Ghanaian president's ideas about the necessity for unity and the political structure most suitable for accomplishing this goal.

The book has an intrinsic value, despite what Dennis Austin considered a mixture of incoherent arguments.[107] Some felt that it was premature, even presumptuous, to distribute this work here at Addis Ababa. It was as if Nkrumah once again wanted to do political marketing, to push a product containing his historical and political theories. In this lofty room, diplomacy was not invariably in step with good manners.

The debates were heated. In a long and robust speech, in keeping with his impressive girth, Botsio unveiled the request of his country and government. It came down to the immediate creation of a unitary African government with a parliament, a foreign policy, a monetary zone and central bank, a defense, citizenship, and a development plan, all held in common by all the states. In his eyes, this proposal was logical and appropriate for the conditions in Africa. The Ghanaians did not want a permanent secretariat in service of the heads of state but rather an executive branch superseding the decisions of individual leaders. Purely and simply, the proposal aimed at the abolition of the existing states and the creation of a supranational entity capable of assuring Africa's development and influence. But did the other ministers understand it in this way?

In the speeches that followed, the heads of other delegations came out against the Ghanaian proposition which, while certainly generous, was romantic and unrealistic. For many it was too radical and dangerous, since it contained the seeds of autocracy and dictatorship at a continental scale. It was not a question of creating a federation of popular African socialist republics, it would seem. Most leaders, like Selassie, recommended a slow and functional approach. At most, they desired the creation of some working institutions limited to continental affairs. If there was to be an organization of unity, they thought, it could only act as a framework for discussion.

It came as no surprise that on all points on the agenda, the arguments advanced by Ghana were rejected, despite Botsio's eloquence and the historical logic of his argument. This defeat confirmed the power of the Monrovia group whose member countries were by far in the majority at this conference, and which claimed to take a pragmatic approach. And, it should be added, this realism was not limited to so-called moderate countries. Ghana's proposal also did not obtain unanimity within the Casablanca group. In sum, for nearly five years Nkrumah's African policy had been deployed in a direction opposite to that of the evolution of the newly independent African states. Ghana was alone, and no one subscribed to its ideas.

Then the Ghanaian delegation resorted to extortion. It declared that President Nkrumah would not attend the conference if his proposal was not accepted. The feeling in the room was that it was regrettable that it had come to this. Attend or don't attend, that's Nkrumah's business, exclaimed some delegates behind the scenes. No one was fooled. Each knew that the question of unity was Kwame Nkrumah's passion and that he could not let such an occasion, grandiose and historical as it was, pass him by. The extortion did not work. Indeed, the leader whose name is identified with the modern saga of unity arrived in Addis Ababa on May 19 amid a cheering crowd and before an audience of dignitaries with Emperor Haile Selassie at its head.

Nkrumah had the time to contact many delegations and above all to feel the pulse of the conference itself. Thus, he learned about the failure of the conference of ministers of foreign affairs and about the creation of a special subcommittee, including Ghana, responsible for writing a preamble meant for the heads of state. For the Ghanaian leader, despite the failure of his minister of foreign affairs, the die had not yet been cast and there was one last chance. It was up to him now, as a theorist and strategist, to use his words to make the best of the situation. To attain his goals, on May 24, 1963, he presented a long, impassioned speech, true to his dream.

NKRUMAH BEFORE AFRICA

In the conference's great hall of honor, there was a solemn moment when Kwame Nkrumah rose to take the floor before his peers. Some admired him; others doubted his sincerity and opposed him. All eyes were turned on him; known to nearly everyone, he was famous across the continent. He was a hero. Turning his thoughts beyond his peers and the crowd of spectators, he thought of Africa, of its many, complex problems and its future. He considered the generations to come that would have to judge the actions of the conference that he was about to address. The powerful current of history uniting Africans carried him away and gave him the heart to formulate his hopes.

By virtue of his intellectual bent, Nkrumah meticulously prepared his arrival at Addis Ababa. Since January 1963, when the newspaper *Spark* "addressed the conscience of Africans," he wanted to break his isolation and to make his vision of unity agreeable to most leaders. His envoys traversed the various capitals to present his criticism of the ideas of Liberia and Ethiopia. At Flagstaff House, the presidential residence, Barden, Tettegah, Dei-Anang and other intimate advisers gave him the impression that unity was possible.

Along the same lines, Nkrumah formulated a concrete and concise plan for political unification. He sent copies of it to the other heads of state to serve as a framework for discussion at Addis. To avoid the old quarrels, this document emphasized the merit of both the Monrovia and Casablanca groups for having considered the question of the moment, African unity. In April, his ambassador at Addis Ababa, Ebenezer Debrah, submitted the agenda "For the creation of the political union of African states" to the Ethiopian minister of foreign affairs, and he asked for it to be included in the conference program. The Ghanaian leader left nothing to chance.

As for his address, Nkrumah constructed his speech to reflect thoughts that originated in his years of study. He organized it so that it clearly expressed the essential point of his program. As an address rooted in the past and present but geared toward the future, the speech would be historic and educational, the tone moderated and subtle in its wording, the content pragmatic. These qualities helped to make it eloquent, powerful, and accessible to the ordinary listener.

The speech bears closer examination. It is poorly known in Francophone Africa. After the customary salutations and a clear and precise introduction, the speaker got straight to the heart of the matter. Speaking frankly, he emphasized the urgent necessity of the day's agenda: "Our objective is African union now. There is no time to waste. We must unite now or perish."[108] A fine rhetorician, Nkrumah adopted this categorical and imperative tone to capture his audience from the start. The message must have burst like a bomb, leaving no doubt in the minds of the crowd which was riveted on him. By speaking directly, this method aimed at producing the maximum results with a minimum of words. Rather revolutionary, this technique surprised the audience, accustomed as it was to emphatic turns of phrase.

The second part of the address, long and historical, seemed like a reflection on African nationalism and his fight against colonialism. With pride, Nkrumah recalled this heroic struggle. He explained how the victory over colonialism demanded the redoubling of energy for an action that was equally grand and urgent—the struggle for unity:

> A whole continent has imposed a mandate upon us to lay the foundation of our union at this conference. It is our responsibility to execute this mandate by creating here and now, the formula upon which the requisite superstructure may be erected.... No sporadic act nor pious resolution can resolve our present problems. Nothing will be of avail, except the united act of a united Africa.[109]

For Nkrumah the pan-Africanist, it was not only history that demanded unity, but also the current challenge in Africa thrown by modern imperialism. As he saw it, the independence of all nations was threatened, and the only logical response to this domination was found in solidarity before the common enemy. And so, he forcefully declared in an unfailingly direct tone:

> The unity of our continent, no less than our separate independence, will be delayed if, indeed, we do not lose it, by hobnobbing with colonialism. African unity is, above all, a political kingdom which can only be gained by political means. The social and economic development of Africa will come only within the political kingdom, not the other way round. The United States of America, the Union of Soviet Socialist Republics, were the political decisions of revolutionary peoples before they became mighty realities of social power and material wealth.[110]

Then, like an instructor in economics, Nkrumah analyzed the process of Africa's economic exploitation, and its consequent impoverishment. The continent's wealth in various agricultural and mineral resources seemed to him the material basis for unity, as well as a basis for the improvement of living conditions for African peoples. With a magisterial eloquence that could put some audiences to sleep, he emphasized the economic reasons that kept Africa under imperialist domination.

To conclude this section, he invited his peers to recall once again the lessons of the struggle of American revolutionaries against the emerging imperialism of the past two centuries. The maturity of imperialism, he added, demanded from that day forward that we "come together in the African unity that alone can save us from the clutches of neo-colonialism."[111] In a very fitting manner, this image foretold the conditions of Africa today.

The depth and gravity of reflection give this speech special merit. The author conceived his address with wisdom and shrewdness that led to a paradigm worthy of the attention of today's best thinkers. In this respect, the speech retains a strong pertinence, in this African world still combatting the resurgence of economic difficulties and the delay in technology that is remaking the world:

> We have the resources. It was colonialism in the first place that prevented us from accumulating the effective capital; but we ourselves have failed to make full use of our power in independence to mobilize our resources for the most effective take-off into thorough-going economic and social development.... We shall accumulate machinery and establish steel works, iron foundries and factories; we shall link the various states of our continent with communications by land, sea and air. We shall cable from one place to another, phone from one place to the other and astound the world with our hydroelectric power; we shall drain marshes and swamps, clear infested areas, feed the undernourished, and rid our people of parasites and disease....
>
> We shall harness the radio, television, giant printing presses to lift our people from the dark recesses of illiteracy. A decade ago, these would have been visionary words, the fantasies of an idle dreamer. But this is the age in which science has transcended the limits of the material world, and technology has invaded the silences of nature.... We cannot afford to pace our needs, our development, our security, to the gait of camels and donkeys.[112]

The idea is pertinent and the image beautiful. This passage should be understood considering the gulf that was carved out day by day between the industrialized and non-industrialized worlds. One, driven by science and the will to conquer the universe, is continuously advancing and creating. The other revels in its cumbersome nature, its traditions, and archaic and ineffective structures. To paraphrase one author, Africa seemed like an old-fashioned mother, infatuated with old things.

The continent had yet to enter the twenty-first century. At Addis Ababa, Kwame Nkrumah's voice sounded like that of a visionary determined to usher his world into the era of the great technological revolution, the source of progress. The need to satisfy these imperatives and, we should add, to reduce the risks of fratricidal wars between both states and ethnic groups, demanded unity. This was his message to his peers, and above all to the Africa of his day and the days to come.

In the last part of his address, Nkrumah presented his plan for the construction "of Africa by Africans themselves and for Africans." Thus, he sincerely and loudly expressed his thought:

> Unite we must. Without necessarily sacrificing our sovereignties, big or small, we can, here and now forge a political union based on defense, foreign affairs and diplomacy, and a common citizenship, and an African currency, an African Monetary Zone and an African Central Bank. We must unite in order to achieve the full liberation of our continent.... We have been charged with this sacred task by our own people, and we cannot betray their trust by failing them....

> No independent African State today by itself has a chance to follow an independent course of economic development, and many of us who have tried to do this have been almost ruined or have had to return to the fold of the former colonial rulers. This position will not change unless we have unified policy working at the continental level. The first step towards our cohesive economy would be a unified monetary zone....

> The hour of history which has brought us to this assembly is a revolutionary hour. It is the hour of decision.... The masses of the people of Africa are crying for unity. The people of Africa call for the breaking down of the boundaries that keep them apart.... They understand that only its realization [of unity] will give full meaning to their freedom and our African independence.

> It is this popular determination that must move us on to a Union of Independent African States. In delay lies danger to our well-being, to our very existence as free states. It has been suggested that our approach to unity should be gradual, that it should go piece-meal. This point of view conceives of Africa as a static entity with 'frozen' problems which can be eliminated one by one.... This view takes no account of the impact of external pressures. Nor does it take cognizance of the danger that delay can deepen our isolations and exclusiveness; that it can enlarge our differences and set us drifting further and further apart into the net of neo-colonialism, so that our union will become nothing but a fading hope, and the great design of Africa's full redemption will be lost, perhaps, forever... .

I have spoken at some length, Your Excellencies, because it is necessary for us all to explain not only to one another present here but also to our people who have entrusted to us the fate and destiny of Africa. We must therefore not leave this place until we have set up the effective machinery for achieving African Unity.[113]

This then is a brief summary of President Kwame Nkrumah's address at Addis Ababa. His speech ranks among the greatest speeches in the history of African interstate conferences. The ideas were familiar since he had been spreading them in all arenas since the Manchester Conference eighteen years before. What gave this speech a particular allure was not the novelty of its theme or the ardor of the orator, but rather the constant and calm references to African peoples. It was to this vast audience, not present at Addis Ababa, that the speaker gave priority, as if trying to communicate with his peers would be a dialogue of the deaf.

Indeed, numerous leaders preceded Nkrumah at the podium. Despite their differences, none of them proclaimed the urgency of political unity on an institutional basis in a persuasive way. They were in favor of unity, but what kind of unity? This was the question.

Overall, they preferred an African union centered on meetings and consultations, held regularly between heads of state, but no coordination on issues of foreign, economic, or social policy. As Glélé-Ahanhanzo has quite aptly written, very few African leaders in fact thought to give priority to Africa and to the development of African unity. At best, each thought of the survival of his own people, or if not, at least the consolidation of his own power and the permanence of his own sovereign state.[114] Whether it was modelled after the Arab League which Nasser proposed or that of the American states, it was an affair of a union of presidents rather than a union placed at the service of the governed peoples. This was the problem of the OAU from its creation up to today; and it was the cause of its failure.

This is perhaps why Nkrumah preferred to speak to Africa itself. Was it not preferable to serve as the voice and conscience of the people? One could say that that was the role of an apostle. In the opinion of most observers, Nkrumah's speech impressed the entire room. But he could not persuade the Caesars assembled before him. His demands seemed excessive, and they did not want to set aside their crowns. And so, the speaker gave the mission of building unity back to the people. This tactic made the address prophetic and revolutionary.

NKRUMAH AND THE OAU

Adu Boahen and other writers considered the creation of the Organization of African Unity on May 25, 1963 a deliberate affront to Nkrumah.[115] This evaluation seems somewhat excessive. What is certain is that the OAU did not correspond to the dream of the Ghanaian leader. The creation of African unity with a federal government was postponed indefinitely. In this respect, Addis Ababa was a great defeat for Nkrumah. The remaining question was how would he react in the face of the new context that emerged from the aftermath of Addis Ababa?

To answer this question, it is useful to examine the charter of the organization. The OAU's objectives are clearly stated in article II. The OAU aims to: 1) promote unity and solidarity among African states; 2) coordinate and intensify cooperation and efforts to improve the living conditions of Africans; 3) defend their sovereignty, territorial integrity, and independence; 4) eliminate colonialism in all its forms; and 5) strengthen international cooperation.

The "founding fathers" of the OAU were undoubtedly resolved to assure the primacy of the state over that of the association. The organization was only a simple continental instrument in the service of the heads of state. It had only those rights granted by them, and they granted rights very parsimoniously. This point is essential. No one must have been mistaken about it, even if the OAU appeared indispensable to some of them. Thus, the charter stressed the necessity for cooperation instead of integration. In other words, the states remained sovereign and immovable.

In conformity with article III, the OAU's existence hinged on the adherence of all partners to the following principles: 1) sovereign equality of all member states; 2) non-interference in the domestic affairs of member states; 3) respect for the sovereignty and territorial integrity of each state and its inalienable right to independent existence; 4) peaceful settlement of disputes by negotiation, mediation, conciliation or arbitration; 5) condemnation without reserve of political assassination and subversive activities by neighboring states or any other state; 6) absolute dedication to the cause of total emancipation for not yet independent countries; and 7) affirmation of the policy of non-alignment with regard to all blocs.

The principles enumerated here represent the ideas fought for so long by Prime Minister Tafawa Balewa, Presidents Tubman and Houphouët-Boigny and their colleagues in the Monrovia group. They wanted to preserve the status quo, including the borders left by colonialism. They were the winners of Addis. For their part, the leaders of the Casablanca group had no complaints. Indeed, despite their connection to Nkrumah, their heart was not in solidarity with the idea of a supranational government.

This third article, which thus won unanimity, contradicted Nkrumah's entire vision. Except for the sixth and perhaps the seventh principle, none of the provisions can be reconciled with the stance that made his name famous. Could he thus be content solely with the requirement to aid liberation movements? Could Africans not unite on other fundamental principles? These questions continued to bother him. Despite everything, it was opportune that cooperation between the African states privileged the question of the continent's total liberation. For many years, the OAU would be known above all for its policy of aiding liberation movements.

At the end of article VII, the OAU's institutions were: 1) an assembly of the heads of state and government; 2) a council of ministers; 3) a general secretariat; and 4) a commission for mediation, reconciliation, and arbitration. The assembly which in principle gathered once per year was the supreme mechanism of the OAU; its important resolutions required a two-thirds majority vote. The council of ministers of foreign affairs gathered twice yearly and in an extraordinary session was responsible for planning the conferences.

As for the general secretariat, the heads of state elected it. The general secretariat directed the organization's affairs in accordance with the instruction of the heads of state and with the assistance of the under-secretaries. The general secretary and his staff were forbidden from seeking out and receiving instructions from any government. It is not necessary to further detail the OAU's numerous commissions and other secondary features.

Since the charter adopted by the other heads of state was far from corresponding to his plan, observers wondered if Nkrumah would agree to sign it. As a matter of integrity, many of his advisers and especially officials from the Bureau of African Affairs opposed signing it. The latter thought that the OAU would perhaps disintegrate because of its contradictions. In contrast, the Ghanaian diplomats, despite their dissatisfaction, urged their country to participate in this interstate organization to prevent its isolation and even to relaunch, later, the president's ideals. After all, the charter could be revised.

Nkrumah the politician understood the necessity of compromise as a condition for realizing his ulterior plans. But the factor that seems to have determined his position more than any other was the influence of Emperor Haile Selassie, for whom he never concealed his admiration. Indeed, how would one resist the powerful symbol of pan-Africanism that Ethiopia represented in 1936? This sentiment left an impression on the former student of the Gold Coast in Pennsylvania and future president of Ghana. After long discussions with the grand host of the conference, Haile Selassie, Nkrumah signed the charter on May 26.

This was a great relief for the other heads of state. African unity was confirmed, and henceforth Africa could speak with one voice, they thought. But how long would this euphoria last? The events that occurred between May 1963 and February 1966 would help clarify the situation in one way or another.

On returning to Accra, Nkrumah gave the impression of being satisfied with the accomplishments of the conference at Addis Ababa and with the realization of "his life's dream," as he declared to parliament. Was this not a strategy at once defensive and offensive? What is undeniable is that he was still holding fast to his plan. He would therefore try to exploit to the fullest the events that arose on the African scene.

Indeed, the first year of the OAU coincided with the rise of socialism in Ghana, renewed sabotage by the opposition and other crises which hardened Nkrumah's domestic and foreign policy. And so, the latent conflict between Accra and Addis Ababa was openly declared on the issues of the general secretariat, liberation movements and refugees.

At the time of their leave-taking, the heads of state entrusted a temporary general secretariat with the task of managing the OAU's affairs until the implementation of the charter. This secretariat was assisted by a committee of experts whose members were chosen from the delegations of Congo-Brazzaville, Ghana, Nigeria, Niger, Uganda, and Egypt. For the Ghanaians, this committee was a commission tasked with re-examining the charter's various proposals. Obviously, Ethiopia was not in agreement and immediately claimed the right to establish the provisional secretariat. Between Accra and Addis, there was a dance of telegrams to settle the situation.

To make a long story short, Nkrumah tried to postpone the implementation of the secretariat and the nomination of the secretary general. Paradoxically, Nigeria's minister of foreign affairs, Jaja Wachuku, supported Ghana's movements since his country desired to be the seat of the OAU. Ghana and Nigeria were again the only two states to express objections to naming Telli Diallo as head of the OAU. In short, to use Thompson's well phrased expression, Nkrumah sought to win through the small door what he had lost through the large one.[116]

The Ghanaian leader fought against the OAU on another front, and this a more sensible one. The exclusion of Ghana from the liberation committee was an insult that Ghanaians could not stomach. How could Modibo Keïta of Mali, who was entrusted with naming the nine committee members, forget Ghana, which had done so much for the cause? Ghana's interference in the affairs of its neighbors, the tension between certain leaders of liberation movements and the Bureau of African Affairs, and Nkrumah's strong personality—all of this could explain the reason for excluding Ghana. But did this justify his position? To express its discontent that June, Accra refused to disburse its contribution to the committee's budget.

On the other hand, the daily paper *Spark* dedicated issues to the OAU's weakness in general and the committee's weakness in particular, which seemed to it to be "manipulated by imperialism." As proof, Ghanaians pointed at the proposal to come to the aid of Roberto Holden of Angola, whom Mobutu and the CIA supported. In the name of the African revolution, Ghana decided to lend aid directly to liberation movements without passing through the intermediary of the OAU. This was a serious affront that had repercussions.

Following the conference at Addis Ababa, the Ghana-Guinea-Mali Union crumbled. Nkrumah thought that other regional organizations should follow suit. And so, he pressured the OAU to declare itself against the African and Malagasy Common Organization (*Organization Commune Africaine et Malgache*-OCAM), which operated under Houphouët-Boigny's influence as well as against the project of a federation of East African states. This action set Tanzania against Ghana and contributed to a tarnishing of Nkrumah's image in East Africa, where he had previously held an exceptional standing. Ghana's last battle against the OAU concerned the right of political refugees to lead attacks against their governments. On this question, Nkrumah failed to influence his peers. Again, he lost a little bit of his prestige.

Faithful to his dream, the Ghanaian leader took advantage of the OAU summits to try to attain his goals. In 1964, numerous events rocked Africa. Border wars broke out between Algeria and Morocco and between Ethiopia and Somalia; France was intervening in Gabon; and British soldiers were putting an end to mutinies in East Africa. For Nkrumah, all this confirmed the need to implement a military high command in the service of the OAU and to revise the charter to institute a continental government. The first OAU summit at Cairo in July 1964 was well timed.

As usual, Ghana sent a large delegation to Cairo. President Nkrumah forcefully laid out his propositions to the assembly of state leaders. Obviously, they were all rejected, including the decision to contribute to the liberation committee funds. This was a defeat,

or rather, a humiliation. Most state leaders no longer tolerated
Nkrumah's obstinacy. Julius Nyerere of Tanzania, who had admired
him not long ago, nevertheless abruptly addressed him: "Mr. President, go ahead and unite with yourself."[117] Nkrumah would not
budge. Sékou Touré did not hide his impatience and drily responded
to him, the Kwame who was his generous partner in 1958: "there is
no question of a unitary government."[118]

Julius Nyerere of Tanzania and Kwame Nkrumah of Ghana.

With the disaster of Cairo, the influence of the radical left skyrocket-
ed in Accra. The Bureau of African Affairs saw its prerogatives grow
to the detriment of those of the minister of foreign affairs. The Bureau was authorized to redouble its assistance to refugees who desired
to overthrow their regimes.

With the help of foreign experts from countries of the east, training camps multiplied in Ghana, such as in Mampong (north of Kumase), Half-Assini near the Ivorian border, and of course the famous Camp Obenimase on the road between Accra and Kumase. Côte d'Ivoire, Upper Volta, Togo, Cameroon, Senegal, Niger, and Nigeria were the targets of subversive activities. As if to confront a problem head-on, Houphouët-Boigny publicly threatened to boycott the Accra summit in 1965 if Ghana did not expel the refugees and renounce subversion. Meanwhile, to calm the tension and save the summit, Tafawa Balewa held an extraordinary conference of the ministers of foreign affairs at Lagos in June 1965. In a collective outcry, everyone condemned Nkrumah and demanded that he reconcile his African policy with the spirit of the OAU.

Since he acknowledged the importance of the summit, Nkrumah tried to make amends. But he could not satisfy Houphouët and his colleagues in the Council of Accord (Conseil de l'entente). Consequently, the member states of this regional organization, as well as Togo, Gabon, Chad, and Madagascar, refused to participate in the summit of Accra in October 1965, which normally should have enhanced Nkrumah's glory. Some rebuked the absent parties themselves for failing to respect the OAU's spirit of collaboration and dialogue. Whatever the case, the summit was a complete fiasco. Accra symbolized the collapse of the African policy of President Nkrumah, a captain unable to lead his vessel through the African storm. He emerged weakened and isolated, disillusioned, and bitter.

Forever intrepid, on December 16, 1965, Nkrumah broke diplomatic relations with Great Britain after the unilateral declaration of independence by Ian Smith, leader of the white minority government of South Rhodesia (Zimbabwe). This courageous decision regilded his image in African revolutionary circles. Tireless, the visionary leader would exert himself to rebuild his prestige anew, not on the African scene but in Asia, by mediating the Sino-Soviet conflict. This was another dream. But his officers, aided by the CIA, understood how to take advantage of his absence and his weaknesses to put an end to his rule, on February 24, 1966.

Truly a dramatic conclusion! Kwame, Saturday's child, seemed to have been called to follow and irresistibly suffer the path already drawn for his future. For, in Akan cosmogony, Saturday was the day of great celebrations—funerals, sacrifices, prayers, and pilgrimages to the sacred woods. It was a fateful day. According to this belief, every boy born on this day would perhaps have great exploits but would also perhaps suffer a tragic fall.

After seven years of exile and reflection, of leading a simple but intellectually active and edifying life at Villa Sylli in Conakry, Guinea, the great dreamer of modern Africa died, weakened by cancer, at a treatment facility in Bucharest, Romania, on April 27, 1972.[119] Before passing, however, he left a bright beacon of hope for Africa in unity and prosperity for generations to come.

Kwame Nkrumah Mausoleum, site of Nkrumah's grave, located in downtown Accra, Ghana.

CONCLUSION

Map of contemporary Africa

This book has described some of the epic phases of Kwame Nkrumah's struggle for the independence of his country, Ghana, and the unity of his continent, Africa. Two gigantic, complex, and intricate tasks indeed. Each separately was Promethean in scope, and perhaps beyond the capacity of a single leader, however able and determined he was. Yet, Nkrumah dared and endeavored. He succeeded in attainting Ghana's independence. Africa's unity proved more difficult, the road being bumpier and harsher. For trying, Nkrumah earned a place among the great figures of modern Africa, his beloved world.

Nkrumah's intentions were blameless, comprehensive, and honorable. Almost like a pilgrim, he traveled to diverse countries, and spread the gospels of his cherished thoughts of African independence and unity. He also welcomed many more visitors to Accra. To him, the matter was sacrosanct. Still, he made foes within his country and abroad. He experienced adversity in various forms: poverty in his schooling, jealousy in political struggle, and other hardships that bolstered his sense of pride and dignity and his commitment to freedom and unity.

Nkrumah experienced the meanness and bitter ugliness of jail for the cause of freedom and dignity. He successfully achieved his first dream, on March 6, 1957, when he and his fellow compatriots hoisted the red, yellow, and green flag of Ghana. Colonization then was at its peak in Africa and Asia. Nkrumah's achievement, an impressive accomplishment, was a well-deserved feat in a well-endowed and well-managed territory. Under his leadership, the future of Ghana loomed high and bright, with a robust foreign reserve. Its national hero, Kwame Nkrumah, could seek to implement his second dream, the quest for Africa's continental unity.

Continental unity was a vision hard to construct and implement, however. Africa is not a country, but an assortment of countries, states, peoples, and cultures that underwent, for the most part, various colonial traditions. The lack of infrastructures, coupled with poverty, poor education, and other factors of underdevelopment, further exacerbated the conditions. Unity appeared difficult to realize in a short time, contrary to Nkrumah's dream. Most leaders underscored this reality in their speeches in Addis Ababa.

The President trusted the power and feasibility of his dream. He truly believed in the will to dare, plan, and carve a system. Such a modus operandi somehow conformed to the cosmology of the Akan milieu, in which he was born and raised. Was he not *Kwame*, a son of Saturday? It was believed such a man may hold and realize great and noble visions.

Yet, all projects are not doable, when the negotiations entail numerous strong-willed leaders like in the Addis Ababa conference room where the African heads of state held their talk. In such gatherings, destinies and resolves often coalesce and vie. Kwame Nkrumah assumed the path of progress could lead to a favorable conclusion that foretold growth for Africans. Hence, he strived as much he could and until the end.

Beginning in 1958, Kwame Nkrumah argued for a large-scale unity that would result in even greater liberty and pride for Africa. Auspiciously, Nkrumah, a groundbreaker with a dream unmatched on the global African scene, then held a large war chest. The funds could enable him to finance his vision—Ghana's foreign reserves surpassed those of India. What an amazing position. Independently, he funded most of his projects of unity, thanks to the revenues from Ghana's production of cocoa and other exports. Having the means to further his politics, he could boast of his determination, when many countries still lacked basic infrastructures. He needed no external funding from former colonizers and few peers could realistically compete against him.

Not surprisingly, Nkrumah convened his colossal continental meetings in Accra, financed African liberation movements, and befriended the emerging leaders of such movements. These efforts spread Ghana's name and Nkrumah's own mystique. But they also prompted several African leaders to question his objective intentions, while paying lip service to the question of African unity. His continuous criticism of colonialism, Portugal, South African apartheid, and other remnants of colonialism—British, French and Portuguese—began to vex the leading Western countries, even some African leaders, and the U.N. General Secretariat. His ideological stubbornness tarnished his image, taxed his persona, and finally created the conditions for his failure. Tragically, Nkrumah could unite with none. Neither neighboring Côte d'Ivoire, Togo nor Benin nor even supposedly friendly Guinea, Mali and Tanzania embraced Ghana's path.

Nkrumah annoyed other African leaders by his persistence on the establishment of unity. He was undoubtedly ahead of his peers. Yet no other leader embraced his plan and gave up the sovereignty of his state for a dream—though one of African unity. On this front, he swallowed a bitter pill, and he remained with his mind overflowing with drafts of articles of unification. He was alone to dance the high-life tune of unity and solidarity to which he had dedicated so much of his life.

Realistically, the dream of continental unity in Africa was a vision hard to fulfill, given underdevelopment, the want of infrastructures and other preconditions. Yet, such a dream could be a source of tragedy. Nkrumah firmly testified to the principle of the struggle between foretold community-based wisdom and destiny, and individually-motivated resolve. These two forces often converge or compete with one another. Kwame Nkrumah assumed, once more, that the path and achievement of progress depended on the merger of these two ideas. And the child from Nkroful unfalteringly endeavored in his dream until the end.

This book has shown that Nkrumah's politics of unity stemmed in part from a consciousness of critical past events performed by the earlier generations and deeds endured together by the living. Such politics also originated from the will to act with others together for a common goal. Politics is indeed rooted in the awareness of the past, the present and the future, and as such might serve as a dynamic force of growth and development. This was Nkrumah's conviction and plan for Africa. Though Nkrumah could not convince his peers about the urgency of a common goal that might be beneficial to the welfare of all, he remained unwavering in his thought that unity was a force of development for the future of Africa.

Since his college years, Nkrumah deeply felt the backwardness and stagnation of Africa in world history and affairs. In his judgment, therefore, unity appeared as a solution for advancement, using the example of the United States, which moved from a colonial state to an advanced liberal modern super-power. While in exile in Guinea, with sadness, he felt the failure of his dream of unity, he lamented the multiplication of coups and border conflicts, and the slow disappearance of African unity itself. He resented this situation. These events, however, testified to the need for African unity.

Headless statue of Kwame Nkrumah. Its head was cut off during the 1966 coup that ousted him from office. The head now lies to the left of the statue.

The OAU charter remained unchanged since 1963. New independent states would join the organization, but Morocco withdrew in

1984 due to the Saharawi crisis. Although the OAU continued to hold regular meetings in Addis Ababa, it lacked effectiveness, and some countries failing to honor their dues. The OAU had become, to quote an author, a "talking shop" with no power to improve the conditions of the African people and solve their urgent needs. Colonel Muamar Gadhafi of Libya, an Arab leader with a rare consciousness of Africanity, intervened. Gadhafi challenged all to make the OAU more relevant and his financial contribution led the OAU at the Sirte Extraordinary Summit in 2001 to reinvent itself with a new name, African Union (AU). South Africa, emerging from apartheid, also contributed by launching the AU in 2002.

Yet, regional conflicts, environmental disasters, pandemics, youth unemployment, immigration, and gender inequality have further revealed the inadequacy of the AU. In other words, the consensus is that the African Union is unable to solve Africa's urgent challenges. At every summit, mostly since 2007 in Accra, the heads of states have considered the issue of an effective AU government that Kwame Nkrumah had forcefully proposed. In conclusion, Nkrumah's vision of African unity has remained a challenge for today's children of the continent.

BIBLIOGRAPHY

Austin, Dennis. *Politics in Ghana.* Oxford, 1964.

Awonoor, Kofi. *The Ghana Revolution.* Brasilia, 1984.

Baulin, Jacques. *La politique africaine d'Houphouët Boigny.* Paris, 1980.

Bénot, Yves. *La mort de Lumumba.* Paris, 1989.

Busia, Kofi. *The Position of the Chief in the Modern Political System of Ashanti.* London, 1951.

Davidson, Basil. *Black Star.* New York, 1974.

Du Bois, W. E. B. *Dusk of Dawn.* New York, 1968.

Glélé-Ahanhanzo, Maurice. *Introduction à l'organisation de l'unité africaine et aux organisations régionales.* Paris, 1986.

Hodgkin, Thomas. *Nationalism in Colonial Africa.* New York, 1957.

Legum, Colin. *Pan-Africanism.* New York, 1962.

Nkrumah, Kwame. *Africa Must Unite.* New York, 1964.

———. *Ghana: The Autobiography of Kwame Nkrumah.* New York, 1971.

———. *Neo-colonialism: Last Stage of Imperialism.* New York, 1965.

———. *The Challenge of the Congo.* New York, 1967.

———. *Revolutionary Path.* New York, 1973.

———. *Class Struggle in Africa.* New York, 1968.

Padmore, George. *Pan-Africanism or Communism?* London, 1956.

Powell, Erica. *Private Secretary (Female)/Gold Coast.* New York, 1984.

Rooney, David. *The Political Kingdom in the Third World.* New York, 1988.

Stockwell, John. *In Search of Enemies.* New York., 1978.

Tevoedjre, Albert. *L'Afrique révoltée.* Paris, 1958.

Thompson, W. Scott. *Foreign Policy of Ghana.* Princeton, 1969.

Welch, Claude K. *Dream of Unity: Pan-Africanism and Political Unification in West Africa*. Ithaca, 1966.

Woronoff, Jon. *West African Wager: Houphouet versus Nkrumah*. Metuchen, 1972.

CHRONOLOGY

July 1900	First pan-African conference at London
21 September 1909	Birth of Kwame Nkrumah
July 1919	Second pan-African conference at Paris
August 1921	Third pan-African conference at Brussels
Summer 1923	Fourth pan-African conference at London and Lisbon
February 1927	Meeting of the League against Imperialism at Brussels
August 1927	Fifth pan-African conference at New York
October 1935	Nkrumah's arrival in the USA to study
June 1945	Nkrumah's return to London
August 1945	Creation of the United Gold Coast Convention (UGCC)
November 1945	Nkrumah's return to Accra
28 February 1948	Riot of former soldiers in Accra; the police open fire.
March 1948	Nkrumah and five other leaders of the UGCC arrested
May 1948	Report of the Watson Commission
December 1948	Henley Coussey Commission for a new constitution
12 June 1949	Nkrumah creates the Convention People's Party (CPP)
January 1950	Campaign of civil disobedience and state of emergency in the Gold Coast
22 January 1950	Nkrumah arrested and condemned to three years in prison
8 February 1951	Legislative elections, triumph of Nkrumah and the CPP
12 February 1951	Nkrumah freed, named head of government
6 March 1957	Independence of Ghana
April 1958	First conference of independent states at Accra

2 October 1958	Independence of Guinea
20 November 1958	Sékou Touré at Accra
23 November 1958	Ghana-Guinea Union
December 1958	First conference of African peoples at Accra
January 1959	Formation of the Federation of Mali
April 1959	Nkrumah in Guinea
May 1959	Formation of the Council of Accord (Conseil de l'entente)
July 1959	Conference of Nkrumah, Touré and Tubman at Sanniquellie
30 June 1960	Independence of Congo (Zaire)
11 July 1960	Lumumba appeals to the U.N.
12 July 1960	Arrival of the first Ghanaian contingents at Leopoldville (Kinshasa)
August 1960	Collapse of the Federation of Mali
September 1960	Meeting of Nkrumah and Houphouët at Half-Assini
November 1960	Nkrumah in Mali
Christmas 1960	Ghana-Guinea-Mali Union
December 1960	Constitution of the Brazzaville Group
January 1961	Constitution of the Casablanca Group
November 1961	Conference of the expanded Brazzaville group; constitution of the Monrovia group
August 1962	Attempt on Nkrumah's life at Kulugungu
13 January 1963	Assassination of Sylvanus Olympio
25 May 1963	Creation of the OAU
July 1964	Summit of Cairo
October 1965	Summit of Accra
26 February 1965	*Coup d'état* in Accra while Nkrumah is in China
27 April 1972	Death of Nkrumah in Bucharest, Romania

Notes

I

1. Basil Davidson, *Black Star* (New York, 1974). This idea is also confirmed in my discussions and correspondence with Davidson in 1988 and 1989.

2. At the time of his departure for the United States, the young Nkrumah was happy to receive this telegram from Azikiwe: "Good-bye. Do not forget to trust in God and in yourself." Cited in Davidson, *Black Star*, p. 30. See also Nnamdi Azikiwe, *My Odyssey* (New York, 1974).

3. See *Dynasteurs*, December 1989; *Valeurs actuelles*, 26 February 1990; *Le Monde*, 28 February 1990; *L'Evénement*, 8 March 1990; *L'Express*, 27 April 1990.

4. See Kwame Nkrumah, *Africa Must Unite* (New York, 1964), and *Neo-Colonialism: Last Stage of Imperialism* (New York, 1965).

5. See Jean Lacouture, *De Gaulle*, vol. 1, ch. 25.

6. See Basil Davidson, *Can Africa Survive?* (New York, 1974).

7. Many authors have tried to demonstrate the American CIA's role in Nkrumah's fall. See, for instance, John Stockwell (former CIA chief of operations in Angola), *In Search of Enemies: A CIA Story* (New York, 1978), 201; Kofi Awonoor, *The Ghana Revolution: Background Account from a Personal Perspective* (Brasilia, 1984), 50-51; David Rooney, *Kwame Nkrumah: The Political Kingdom in the Third World* (New York, 1988), 252-257.

8. See, for example, Thomas Hodgkin, *Nationalism in Colonial Africa* (New York, 1957), a quite remarkable work but erroneous in its appreciation of the foundations of unity.

2

9. Kwame Nkrumah, *Ghana: The Autobiography of Kwame Nkrumah* (New York, 1971), 29.

10. Ibid., 49.

11. The *Almami* Samori Ture entered the Ivory Coast and Northern Ghana. The king of the Asante confederation, Prempeh I, planned to form with him a common front against their respective enemies, the French and English. Samori left a marked impression on the Akan populations of Ghana, as seen in the expression "Samori-nana," which spread everywhere and literally means "the grandson of Samori." By extension it designates any male child full of energy and promise. (Information from Kodjo Yeboah-Sampong, Chicago, June 1990).

12. It is important to recall that President Roosevelt and Prime Minister Churchill had already discussed decolonization during their meeting on the Atlantic in 1942. And in 1947 Truman found no reason to help the English perpetuate their domination in India.

13. See, for example, Milton Friedman and Rose Friedman, *Free to Choose* (New York, 1980).
14. Nkrumah, *Autobiography*, 43.
15. Frantz Fanon later borrowed this phrase for his 1961 book of the same name.
16. W. E. B. Du Bois, *Crisis*, 1899.
17. See Alex Haley, *Roots* (New York, 1976). Robert Hayden's poem "Middle Passage" is drawn from his collection, *A Ballad of Remembrance* (1962), and is a brilliant description of the atmosphere and horrors aboard the slave ships.
18. In his poem "Heritage," Countee Cullen asks the question, "What is Africa to me?" Thus, while recognizing the alienation of blacks, he sings of Africa as a paradise lost.
19. John Blassingame, *The Slave Community* (New York, 1972), ch. 2.
20. Claude McKay, "Outcast," in *American Negro Poetry*, edited by Ama Bontemps (New York, 1963), 28.
21. Langston Hughes, *The Collected Works of Langston Hughes: The poems, 1941-1950*, Vol. 2. (Columbia, 2001), 85.
22. Langston Hughes, "Proem" in *The Collected Works of Langston Hughes: The poems, 1921-1940*, Vol. 1 (Columbia, 2001), 22.
23. Hollis R. Lynch, *Edward Wilmot Blyden: Pan-Negro Patriot, 1832-1912* (London, 1967), vii.
24. Martin Luther King, Jr., "Honoring Dr. Du Bois," preface to Du Bois' autobiography, *Dusk of Dawn: An Essay toward an Autobiography of a Race Concept* (New York, 1968), vii-xvii.
25. Du Bois, *Dusk of Dawn*, 116-117.
26. W. E. B. Du Bois, *Crisis*, February 1919, 166.
27. In the name of the queen, Prime Minister Chamberlain responded immediately in a message to the congress that "the government of Her Majesty was resolved to protect the indigenous races."
28. See Du Bois, *Dusk of Dawn*, Ch. 8.
29. Colin Legum, *Pan-Africanism: A Short Political Guide* (London, 1962), 25.
30. Amady Aly Dieng, *Blaise Diagne, député africain* (Paris, 1990).
31. See Du Bois, *Dusk of Dawn*.
32. For example, *Neptune* of Brussels published an article on pan-Africanism's links to bolshevism.
33. Nkrumah, *Autobiography*, 51.
34. Nkrumah, *Autobiography*, 53.
35. Nkrumah, *Autobiography*, 54.

3

36. With the exception of David Rooney, other historians of Ghana overlook this point. See D. Rooney, *Kwame Nkrumah: The Political Kingdom in the Third World* (New York, 1988), 27.

37. Kwame Nkrumah, *Ghana: The Autobiography of Kwame Nkrumah* (New York, 1971), 65.
38. Dennis Austin, *Politics in Ghana* (Oxford, 1964), 4-5.
39. See Frantz Fanon, *Les damnés de la terre* (Paris, 1961), ch. 1.
40. See Kofi A. Busia, *The Position of the Chief in the Modern Political System of Ashanti* (London, 1951).
41. Indeed, for instance, J. B. Danquah is the brother of Nana Ofori Atta, king of Akyem. Kofi Busia is a member of the reigning family of Wenchi (Wankyi) in the Brong (Bono) not far from the Ivorian frontier; Ako Adjei belongs to the princely family of Accra; Simon Dombo is a prince from the north; Joe Appiah belongs to the great royal clan of Kumase.
42. See Nkrumah, *Autobiography*, 94-95. Nkrumah created numerous newspapers in divergent cities including *The Evening News, The National Times, Talking Drums, Accra Evening News* and *Ghana Statesman*. The CPP had its own forum, *The Spark*.
43. George Padmore, *Pan-Africanism or Communism*, 177.
44. Nkrumah, *Autobiography*, 105.
45. Ex-officio: Latin word denoting someone who is a member of an institution or an organization by virtue of their status or position.
46. Westminster: The seat of the British parliament. The Westminster model is applied to a political regime that is parliamentarian and democratic where the majoritarian party head exercises power as the prime minister.
47. Bob Fitch and Mary Oppenheimer, *Ghana: End of an Illusion* (New York, 1966), 29.
48. Nkrumah, *Autobiography*, 136.
49. Poem written by Fred Sarpong, future editor of the *Daily Graphic*, and often performed by highlife orchestras.
50. Literally, the expression "mate meho" means, "I separate myself, I distance myself" or even "I do not want to be part of." Translation by Kodjo Yeboah-Sampong.
51. Kwame A. Ninsin, "The Nkrumah Government and the Opposition of the Nation-State Unity versus Fragmentation," Institute of African Studies, University of Ghana, May 1985.

4

52. June Milne, *Forward Ever: The Life of Kwame Nkrumah* (London, 1977), 29.
53. See W. Scott Thompson, *Foreign Policy of Ghana* (Princeton, 1969).
54. Ibid., xvii.
55. See, for instance, *Afrique histoire* 5 (1982), Dossier Kwame Nkrumah, by Abdoulaye Bathily and E. O. Apronti.
56. See Jon Woronoff, *West African Wager: Houphouët versus Nkrumah* (Metuchen, 1972). As emerges from this study, Houphouët-Boigny shared this opinion about Nkrumah.

57. Thompson, *Foreign Policy of Ghana*, 25-26.
58. Dr. Obed Asamoah, "Nkrumah's Foreign Policy," Institute of African Studies, University of Ghana, Legon, May 1985.
59. For example, for H. T. Alexander, Nkrumah was a "megalomaniac," as he wrote in his book *African Tight-rope* (Boston, 1966); Conor Cruise O'Brien overlooked Nkrumah's role and that of the Ghanaian contingent in Congo in his work *To Katanga and Black* (New York, 1966); only Erica Powell was an exception in writing of Nkrumah as a "man of vision and courage who made great achievements" in her work *Private Secretary (Female)/Gold Coast* (New York, 1984).
60. See Woronoff, *West African Wager*, 8-12.
61. See *Foreign Affairs* 35, no. 34 (July 1957), 599.
62. Cited in *Fraternité Matin*, Abidjan, 12 March 1965.
63. See Jacques Baulin, *La politique africaine d'Houphouët-Boigny* (Paris, 1980).

5

64. Alex Quaison-Sackey, *Africa Unbound* (New York, 1963), 63.
65. Commonwealth: The term denotes an association for the general well-being of partners pursuing liberty and equality. The "commonwealth" was an interstate and intercontinental union whose members were linked by their allegiance to the British crown and the recognition of the sovereignty of Great Brittan as its head.
66. Kwame Nkrumah, "Speech of Welcome," in *Revolutionary Path* (New York, 1973), 120.
67. Frantz Fanon: Psychiatrist, theorist of the revolution in the third world, originally from Martinique, but a member of the Front de Liberation Nationale (FLN) of Algeria.
68. See Albert Tévoedjré, *L'Afrique révoltée* (Paris, 1958).
69. See *Evening News*, 7 September 1959, Accra.
70. See Lansiné Kaba, *Le Non de la Guinée à De Gaulle* (Paris, 1989).
71. Sékou Touré, *Expérience guinéenne et unité africaine* (Paris, 1961), 213.
72. Ibid., 205.
73. Newspaper of the PDG, *La Liberté*, 4 October 1958, Conakry.
74. *Debates*, Accra, 12 December 1958, vol. 12, p. 388.
75. Ibid.
76. Ibid.
77. See Thompson, *Ghana's Foreign Policy*, 69.
78. Ibid.
79. See "Accords franco-guinéens," *La documentation française, notes et études*, no. 2509, 29 January 1959.
80. See *Ghanaian Times*, Accra, 29 July 1959.
81. Indeed, several movements had chosen residence at Conakry including the Union of Peoples of Cameroon (UPC), led by Félix Moumié; and the Movement for the Liberation of Angola (MPLA), led by Agostinho Neto.
82. See Jacques Baulin, *La politique africaine d'Houphouët-Boigny* (Paris, 1980).

83. Extraordinary Congress of the US-RDA, Bamako, 22 September 1960, government press.

84. *L'Essor*, 14 November 1960, Bamako.

85. Claude E. Welch, *Dream of Unity: Pan-Africanism and Political Unification in West Africa* (Ithaca, 1966), 130, n. 22.

86. Colin Legum, *Pan-Africanism: A Short Political Guide* (London, 1962), 190-92.

6

87. See Kwame Nkrumah, *The Challenge of the Congo* (New York, 1967).

88. Yves Bénot, *La mort de Lumumba* (Paris, 1989), 53.

89. Ibid.

90. Nkrumah, *op. cit.*, 14.

91. Bénot, *op. cit.*, 54.

92. Thomas Kanza, *The Rise and Fall of Patrice Lumumba* (Boston, 1979), 139-44.

93. Arthur Lee Burns and Nina Heathote, *Peace-keeping by U. N. Forces* (New York, 1963), 40.

94. Ibid., 41.

95. Nkrumah, *op. cit.*, 42.

96. Catherine Hoskyns, *The Congo Since Independence* (Oxford, 1964), 221-22, cited in Thompson, *op. cit.*

97. Madeleine Kalb, *The Congo Cables: The Cold War in Africa* (New York, 1982), 50.

98. Anicet Kashamura, *De Mobutu aux colonies* (Paris, 1966), 149, cited in Thompson, *op. cit.*

99. Thompson, *op. cit.*, 140.

100. Through his father, Nkrumah belonged to the Asona clan, whose symbol was the crow. See Nkrumah, *Autobiography*, 6.

7

101. Contrary to what was said on the radio by Tawia Adamafio, Nkrumah was injured.

102. *Horoya*, 22 January 1963.

103. *Evening News*, 15 January 1963.

104. *Horoya*, 16 August 1962.

105. Declaration at the United Nations, October 1962.

106. See Maurice Glélé-Ahanhanzo, *Introduction à l'organisation de l'unité africaine et aux organisations régionales* (Paris, 1986).

107. Dennis Austin, *op. cit.*, 398.

108. See Kwame Nkrumah, "Address to the Conference of African Heads of State and Government, 24th May 1963," in *Revolutionary Path*, 233-34.

109. Nkrumah, *Revolutionary Path*, 234.
110. Nkrumah, *Revolutionary Path*, 235.
111. Nkrumah, *Revolutionary Path*, 238.
112. Nkrumah, *Revolutionary Path*, 238.
113. Nkrumah, *Revolutionary Path*, 240-45.
114. Glélé-Ahanhanzo, *op. cit.*, 23.
115. See Adu-Boahen, "Ghana since Independence," in Prosser Gifford and W. Roger Louis, ed., *Decolonization and African Independence: The Transfers of Power, 1960-1980* (New Haven, 1988), 222.
116. Thompson, *op. cit.*, 237.
117. Ibid., 353.
118. Ibid., 356.
119. During his years of exile at Conakry, as if to confirm his revolutionary and intellectual penchant, President Nkrumah published several works (including *Challenge of the Congo, Class Struggle in Africa, Dark Days in Ghana* and *Revolutionary Path*) and many pamphlets.

INDEX